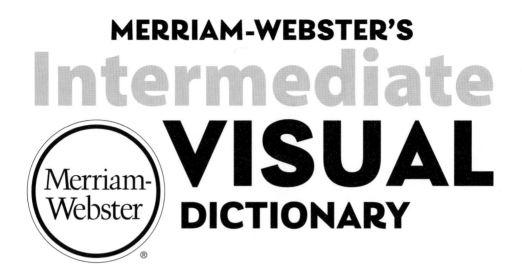

MERRIAM-WEBSTER'S
Intermediate
VISUAL DICTIONARY

Merriam-Webster

MERRIAM-WEBSTER'S
Intermediate
VISUAL DICTIONARY

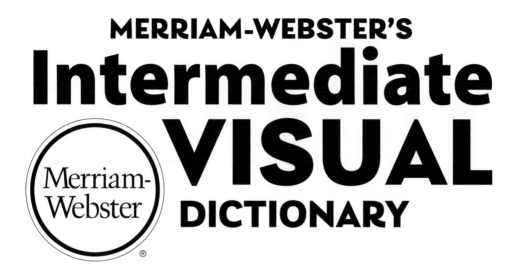

Under the direction of
Jean-Claude **Corbeil**

Merriam-Webster.com

Merriam-Webster, Incorporated
Springfield, Massachusetts
USA

ACKNOWLEDGEMENTS

We would like to thank the following people for their contribution to the various editions of this book:

Jean-Yves Ahern, Danielle Bader, Sophie Ballarin, Stéphane Batigne, Jean Beaumont, Sylvain Bélanger, Manuela Bertoni, Pascal Bilodeau, Marthe Boisjoly, Yan Bohler, Mélanie Boivin, Guy Bonin, Catherine Briand, Julie Cailliau, Myriam Caron Belzile, Érica Charest, Jessie Daigle, Serge D'Amico, Jeanne Dompierre, François Fortin, Margot Froehlich, Éric Gagnon, Jocelyn Gardner, Hélène Gauthier, Catherine Gendreau, Mélanie Giguère-Gilbert, Pascal Goyette, Benoît Grégoire, Guillaume Grégoire, Nathalie Guillo, Any Guindon, François Hénault, Anik Lafrenière, Claude Laporte, Martin Lemieux, Alain Lemire, Rielle Lévesque, Hélène Mainville, Raymond Martin, Émilie McMahon, Philippe Mendes Campeau, Patrick Mercure, Tony O'Riley, Carl Pelletier, Johanne Plante, Sylvain Robichaud, Kathe Roth, Anne Rouleau, Michel Rouleau, Claude Thivierge, Gabriel Trudeau-St-Hilaire, François Turcotte-Goulet, Gilles Vézina, Jordi Vinals, Kathleen Wynd.

QA International would also like to acknowledge the contribution of Jean-Claude Corbeil and Ariane Archambault, the authors of the original terminology of the *Visual Dictionary*, some of which features in this publication.

Finally, we would like to thank most warmly the teachers of Louis-Cyr School Lionel-Groulx College who kindly reviewed the curriculum content in this book.

PUBLISHER
President: Jacques Fortin
CEO: Caroline Fortin
Editorial Director: Martine Podesto

EDITORIAL STAFF
Editor-in-chief: Marie-Anne Legault
Anne-Julie Boucher
Audrey Chapdelaine
Myriam Groulx

ILLUSTRATIONS
Artistic Direction: Anouk Noël
Laurie Pigeon

PRODUCTION MANAGEMENT
Véronique Loranger

LAYOUT, DATABASE AND PREPRESS
Marylène Plante-Germain

PROGRAMMING
John Sebastián Díaz Álvarez

TERMINOLOGY RESEARCH
Carole Brunet

EDUCATIONAL REVIEW
Sébastien Barbeau
Sébastien Gendron
Maxime Lord
Émilie Martin
Sean Mathieu Constantineau
Sandra Pelle
Louis-Philippe Richard

LINGUISTIC REVIEW
English: Idem. Traduction Communication

MERRIAM-WEBSTER EDITORS
Linda Wood
Joan Narmontas
Daniel J. Hopkins

MERRIAM-WEBSTER COVER DESIGN
Joanne K. Lane

MIX
Paper
FSC FSC™ C010615

Merriam Webster is committed to a sustainable future for our business, our readers and our planet. This book is made from Forest Stewardship Council™ certified paper.

ISBN: 978-0-87779-381-6

Merriam-Webster's Intermediate Visual Dictionary was created and produced by:

Merriam-Webster, Inc.

Published by Merriam-Webster, Inc. 2020

© 2020 QA International. All rights reserved.

QA International, a division of
Les Éditions Québec Amérique inc.
7240, Saint-Hubert Street
Montreal (Quebec) H2Y 2E1 Canada
Tel.: 514 499-3000 Fax: 514 499-3010
quebec-amerique.com
qa-international.com

Printed and bound in India. First Printing 2020.
6 5 4 3 2 1 24 23 22 21 20
748 version 1.0.0

Explanatory Chart

Subtheme

Themes are divided into subthemes.

Introduction

A short informative paragraph introduces each subtheme.

Title

The title groups together illustrations of the same subject matter.

Theme

The contents are divided into 10 main themes. The color reference on the outside edge of the page identifies each theme to facilitate quick access to the corresponding section of the book.

74 road transport

The invention of the wheel enabled humans to travel farther and faster, eventually leading to the creation of bicycles, motorcycles and automobiles. Since motorized vehicles first made their appearance in the 19th century, they have not stopped evolving and gaining in popularity. Because of the large numbers of cars on the road, people are now being encouraged to increase their use of public transportation (buses, trains) and ride their bikes when possible to reduce traffic congestion and air pollution.

cycling transport

bicycle/bike

seat · handlebars · brake lever · rear reflector · shifter · front brake · tire pump · headlight · rear brake · spoke · fender · reflector · rack · pedal · water bottle clip · tire · derailleur · tire valve · chain

Transportation

helmet · lock

tool kit · bicycle bag

bike rental
bike repair
bicycle parking
city bicycle
mountain bike
safety vest
bicycle bell
kickstand
inner tube
to ride a bicycle
to brake
to shift gears
to inflate a tire
to fix a flat tire

Term

Each term is listed in the index with a reference to the pages on which it appears. Preference has been given to the singular, except where the use of the plural is more common (in the case of *twins*, for example).

7

Illustration or photo

This serves as a visual reference for each of the associated terms.

road transport   75

public transportation/public transit

bus station
ticket counter
ticket machine
one-way ticket
round-trip ticket
departure time
arrival time
travel time
route
destination
pass
student rate
priority seat
to wait for the bus
to take the bus
to get on the bus
to get off the bus
Does this bus go to…
Which bus goes to…
I would like a ticket for…
I missed my bus.
Can you tell me when we get to…

Transportation

school bus   flashing lights

bus   baggage compartment

bus ticket   stop button

city bus

bus stop   bus shelter   route sign

16 CRIMSON

schedule   passenger   door   driver

Boxes

Boxes enrich the book's content with further words, expressions and key phrases.

Scene

Some terms are depicted in colorful scenes of daily life.

Dotted line

This connects a term to the corresponding part of the illustration or photo.

Contents

The Basics

As life goes on, we encounter different social situations that have their own rules and conventions. When we meet new people, for example, we often use a polite form of address such as Mr. or Ms., but after getting to know them better, we can start calling them by their first names. It is important to know how to behave and communicate, depending on where we are and whom we are talking to.

introduction

to introduce each other   to shake hands

meeting

to greet

new girl

new boy

to feel good

to feel bad

kiss

kiss

hug

bow

Welcome!	What is your name?
Hello!/Hi!	My name is…
Good morning!	Nice to meet you.
Good afternoon!	How are you?
Good evening!	I'm fine, thank you.
Good night!	Where are you from?
Goodbye!	I'm from…
See you soon!	How old are you?
See you tomorrow!	I'm… years old.

The Basics

identity and stages of life

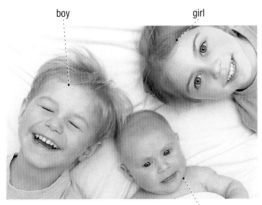

boy

girl

childhood

baby

teenage boy

teenage girl

adolescence (teenage years)

woman

man

schoolboy

schoolgirl

mister/sir

madam/ma'am

adult

working man

working woman

retired

senior citizen

identification paper	Thank you!
passport	You're welcome!
first name	Sorry!
last name	Can you help me?
age	All right.
nationality	I feel sick.
birth date	Where's the toilet?
address	I'm lost.
telephone number	Help!
signature	Watch out!
yes/no	Call emergency services!
Excuse me.	I don't understand.
Please.	Can you repeat?

Figures and numbers as well as time-related expressions are key to learning a new language, because they are used in everyday conversations. "What time is it?" or "What a nice day!" or "What is the weather like?" are questions and expressions we use daily.

The Basics

weather

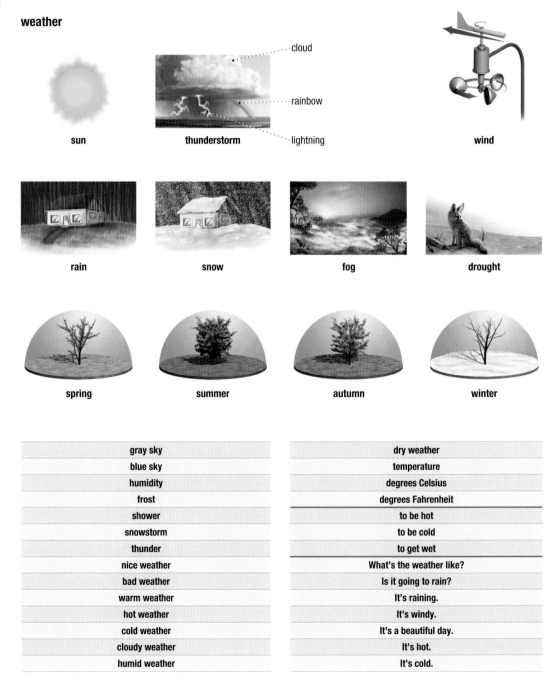

cloud

rainbow

lightning

| sun | thunderstorm | | wind |

| rain | snow | fog | drought |

| spring | summer | autumn | winter |

gray sky	dry weather
blue sky	temperature
humidity	degrees Celsius
frost	degrees Fahrenheit
shower	to be hot
snowstorm	to be cold
thunder	to get wet
nice weather	What's the weather like?
bad weather	Is it going to rain?
warm weather	It's raining.
hot weather	It's windy.
cold weather	It's a beautiful day.
cloudy weather	It's hot.
humid weather	It's cold.

figures and numbers

0	**1**	**2**	**3**
zero	one	two	three
4	**5**	**6**	**7**
four	five	six	seven
8	**9**	**10**	**11**
eight	nine	ten	eleven
12	**13**	**14**	**15**
twelve	thirteen	fourteen	fifteen

sixteen	one hundred
seventeen	one thousand
eighteen	one million
nineteen	one billion
twenty	first
twenty-one	second
twenty-two	third
thirty	fourth
fourty	last
fifty	none/nothing
sixty	few/little
seventy	some
eighty	several
ninety	much/many

The Basics

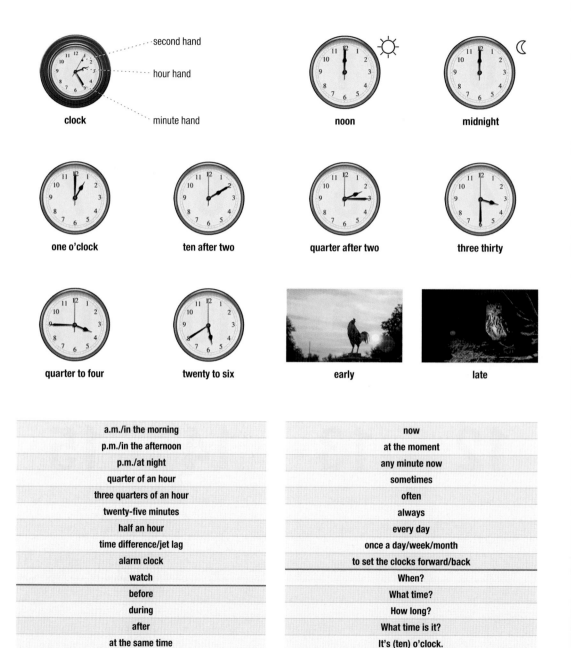

clock

second hand

hour hand

minute hand

noon

midnight

one o'clock

ten after two

quarter after two

three thirty

quarter to four

twenty to six

early

late

a.m./in the morning	now
p.m./in the afternoon	at the moment
p.m./at night	any minute now
quarter of an hour	sometimes
three quarters of an hour	often
twenty-five minutes	always
half an hour	every day
time difference/jet lag	once a day/week/month
alarm clock	to set the clocks forward/back
watch	When?
before	What time?
during	How long?
after	What time is it?
at the same time	It's (ten) o'clock.
since	It's half past (ten).
until	See you later!
later	Right away!
soon	I'll be there soon.
late	I'm early.
on time	I'm late.

day   brightness

night   darkness

year

month

week

MAI – MAY   2019

day

calendar

sunrise   morning   evening   sunset

January	future
February	dawn
March	dusk
April	schedule
May	afternoon
June	yesterday
July	day before yesterday
August	today
September	tomorrow
October	day after tomorrow
November	daily
December	weekly
Monday	monthly
Tuesday	yearly
Wednesday	last/next week
Thursday	last/next month
Friday	last/next year
Saturday	What day is it?
Sunday	What is the date?
past	What is the year?
present	June 4, 2020

Our family members are people we are used to seeing from birth, which is why they greatly influence our characters and values. As we get older, though, we meet many other people: neighbors, friends, teachers and eventually coworkers, not to mention boyfriends or girlfriends. All of them strongly influence our well-being.

Sophia's family

grandfather   grandmother

mother   father   uncle   aunt

cousin   cousin

brother   sister   **Sophia**   spouse

nephew   niece   son   daughter

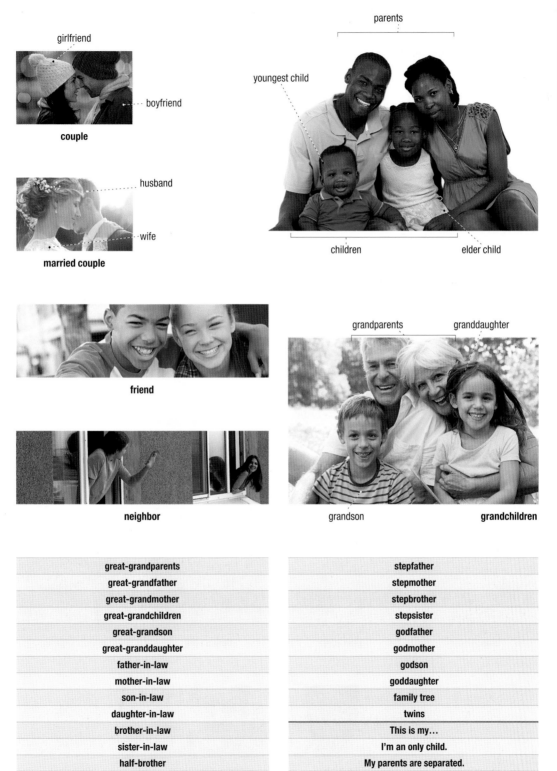

family

girlfriend

boyfriend

couple

husband

wife

married couple

parents

youngest child

children

elder child

The Basics

friend

neighbor

grandparents

granddaughter

grandson

grandchildren

great-grandparents	stepfather
great-grandfather	stepmother
great-grandmother	stepbrother
great-grandchildren	stepsister
great-grandson	godfather
great-granddaughter	godmother
father-in-law	godson
mother-in-law	goddaughter
son-in-law	family tree
daughter-in-law	twins
brother-in-law	This is my…
sister-in-law	I'm an only child.
half-brother	My parents are separated.
half-sister	

Height, skin complexion, eye color… When we first see people we register their physical features. We have no choice over the features we are born with, although we can tweak them a bit with makeup or hairstyles. That is one thing, but characters and emotions are much better indicators of who we are.

physical appearance

········to be young

to be old

age

········to be tall

to be short

height

to wear glasses

to wear braces

to be stout

to be thin

weight

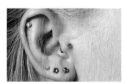

piercing

tattoo

to be muscular

to be slight

blue eyes

green eyes

brown eyes

to wear makeup

to have a beard

to have a mustache

hair

red hair

blond hair

brown hair

black hair

gray hair

white hair

smooth hair

curly hair

wavy hair

to be bald

short hair

long hair

dyed hair

braided hair

ponytail

bun

to be handsome	to have a scar
to be beautiful	to have dimples
to be ugly	to have a mole
to be cute	to have a birthmark
to be pretty	to get wrinkles
to be hairy	My hair is…
to be skinny	My eyes are…
to be fat/obese	I'm… years old.
to be strong	I'm… feet/meter(s) tall.
to be weak	I weigh… pounds/kilograms.
to be elegant	I wear glasses.
to be untidy	I wear contact lenses.
to be tanned	I wear makeup.
to be pale	

The Basics

feelings and personality

to be happy

to be unhappy

to be scared

to be excited

to be angry

to be sad

to be embarrassed

to be proud

to be bored

to be lonely

to be shy

to be self-confident

to be surprised

to be nervous

to be worried

to be depressed

to be stressed

to be disgusted

to be funny

to be serious

to be delighted

to yawn

to be tired

to be exhausted

to be relaxed

The Basics

feelings and personality

to be generous

to be kind

to be grateful

to be disappointed

to be clever

to be confused

to make a face

to wink

to pout

to frown

to smile

to laugh

to cry

to whisper

to shout

to chat

to be honest/dishonest	to be selfish
to be curious	to be friendly
to be patient/impatient	to be amazed
to be tolerant/intolerant	to be indifferent
to be lazy	to be distracted
to be jealous	to sigh
to be calm	I'm satisfied.
to be lucky/unlucky	I'm unsatisfied.
to be polite/impolite	I'm interested.
to be disciplined	I'm not interested.
to be undisciplined	I like…
to be crazy	I don't like…
to be annoyed	I'm in a good mood.
to be silly	I'm in a bad mood.

As with the physical aspects of people, we mainly rely on sight to describe objects or other realities. Is it nearby or is it far away? What color is it? There are many adjectives or qualifiers we can attach to objects to help us define, for instance, their size, position or color. Those words are used regularly to describe things more precisely.

dimensions

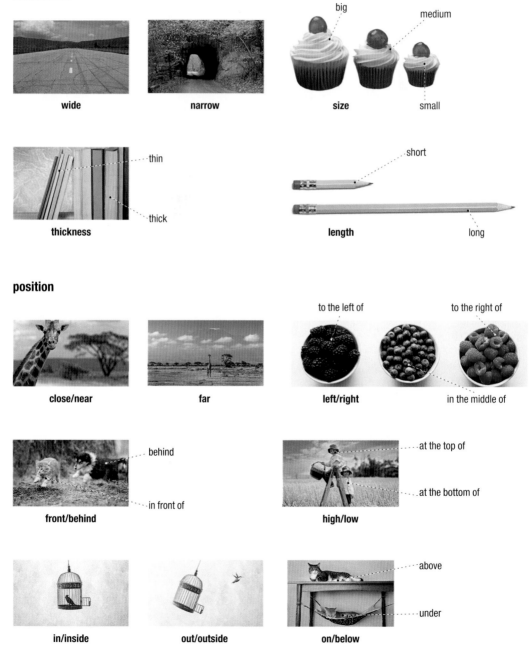

wide   **narrow**   **size** — big / medium / small

thin / thick — **thickness**   **length** — short / long

position

to the left of / to the right of

close/near   **far**   **left/right** — in the middle of

behind / in front of — **front/behind**   at the top of / at the bottom of — **high/low**

in/inside   **out/outside**   above / under — **on/below**

colors

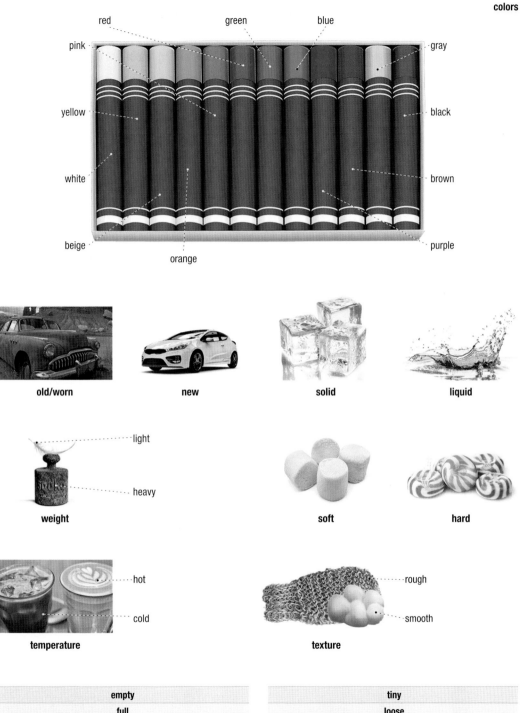

red   green   blue

pink   gray

yellow   black

white   brown

beige   purple

orange

old/worn	**new**

solid	**liquid**

light

heavy

weight

soft   **hard**

hot

cold

temperature

rough

smooth

texture

empty	tiny
full	loose
tidy	tight
untidy	equal/even
light	unequal/uneven
dark	quiet
huge	noisy

The Basics

We learn some skills or actions very early, like talking, eating and walking. They seem so natural that we do them without thinking. Others, like reading, riding a bicycle, or playing a musical instrument take more time and effort to learn. While more difficult to master, they are an important part of our everyday lives and contribute to our development and well-being. Some activities will vary according to individual preferences.

to walk

to run

to jump

to crawl

to be standing

to be sitting

to be lying down

to bend

to talk

to sing

to dance

to carry

to pull

to push

to throw

to catch

to hold

to use a device

to send/receive a message

to search/research

The Basics

to get up

to go to bed

to get dressed

to undress

to brush one's teeth

to brush one's hair

to take a bath

to take a shower

to wash one's hands

to eat

to drink

to sleep

to go to school

to do homework

to read

to write

to draw

to listen to music

to take a picture

to play

to play together	to play a musical instrument
to play cards	to tidy up/clean up
to watch television	I need to go to the bathroom.
to watch a movie	We are going to the cinema.
to play sports	We are going to play…
to play video games	We are going shopping.
to paint	

The Basics

From one culture to another, we celebrate life's important milestones and events differently, whether they be birthdays, anniversaries, successes, weddings or other highlights. Those events are sometimes marked by religious or secular ceremonies. Each one is an occasion to bring family and friends together.

fireworks

New Year

Christmas tree

gift

Christmas

Valentine's Day

Hanukkah

costume

pumpkin

Halloween

Thanksgiving

carnival

brass band

flag

National Day

Ramadan

birth

first day of school

graduation ceremony

moving

to fall in love

engagement

marriage

pregnancy

birthday party

decoration

balloon

piñata

paper garland

party hat

guest

noisemaker

ribbon

confetti

gift bag

birthday cake

gifts

gift wrap

greeting card

candle

public holiday	**separation/divorce**
Mother's Day	**death/funeral**
Father's Day	**Happy birthday!**
Easter	**Happy holidays!**
Yom Kippur	**Congratulations!**
Diwali	**Best wishes!**
Wesak	**My condolences.**

Like the body of most animals, that of humans presents a bilateral symmetry. This means that most parts are duplicated on both the left and the right sides of the body. Even if they are based on the same model, every body is unique. The shape, height and proportions of the human body vary greatly from one person to another.

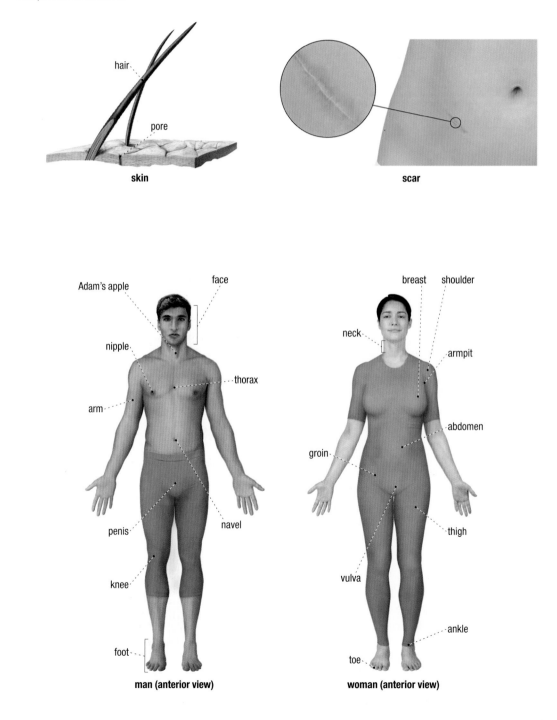

hair

pore

skin

scar

Adam's apple

face

breast   shoulder

nipple

neck

armpit

thorax

arm

abdomen

groin

penis

navel

thigh

knee

vulva

ankle

foot

toe

man (anterior view)

woman (anterior view)

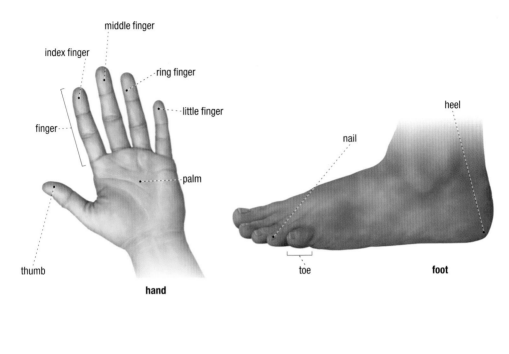

middle finger

index finger

ring finger

little finger

finger

palm

thumb

hand

heel

nail

toe

foot

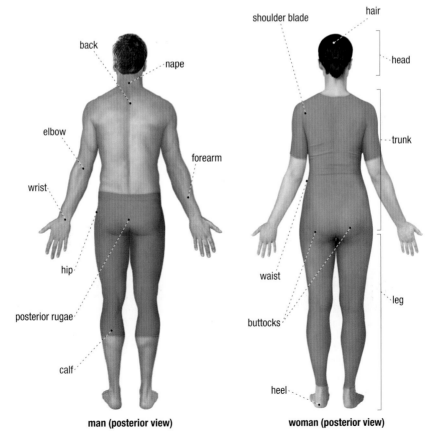

shoulder blade

hair

head

back

nape

trunk

elbow

forearm

wrist

hip

waist

leg

posterior rugae

buttocks

calf

heel

man (posterior view)

woman (posterior view)

Body and Health

anatomy

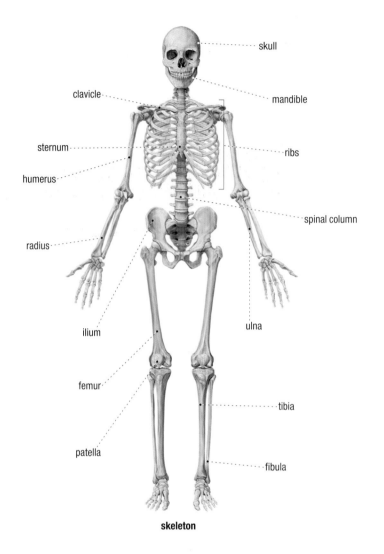

skull

mandible

clavicle

sternum

ribs

humerus

spinal column

radius

ilium

ulna

femur

tibia

patella

fibula

skeleton

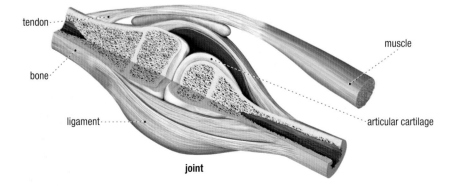

tendon

muscle

bone

ligament

articular cartilage

joint

anatomy

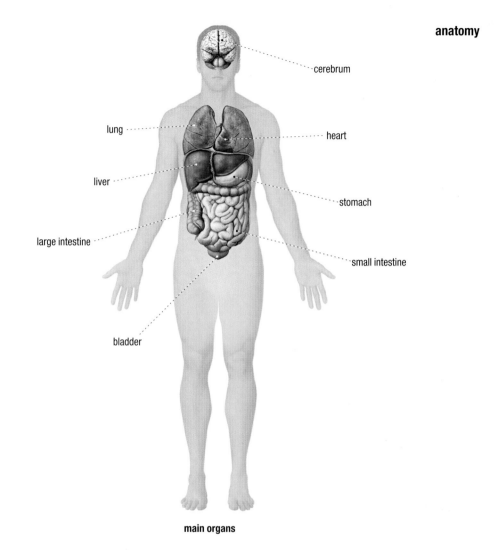

cerebrum

lung

heart

liver

stomach

large intestine

small intestine

bladder

main organs

vertebra	larynx
digestive system	trachea
saliva	bronchial tube
digestion	cardiovascular system
esophagus	blood circulation
pancreas	vein
endocrine system	artery
gland	nervous system
hormone	cerebrum
sweat	spinal cord
respiratory system	nerve
breathing	lymphatic system
pharynx	urinary system
vocal cord	kidney

Medical progress and preventive measures now enable us to prevent or treat a great number of diseases and live much longer than our ancestors. Some accidents and ailments are beyond our control, of course, but sound lifestyles help to keep the body healthy. Those lifestyles include balanced diet and regular exercise.

illness and injuries

to be sick

to treat

wound

injury

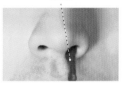

blood

hemorrhage (bleeding)

fever

dizziness

bruise

fracture

cough

redness

burn

sunburn

headache/migraine

acne

itching

insect sting

swelling

edema

blister

wart

doctor's office

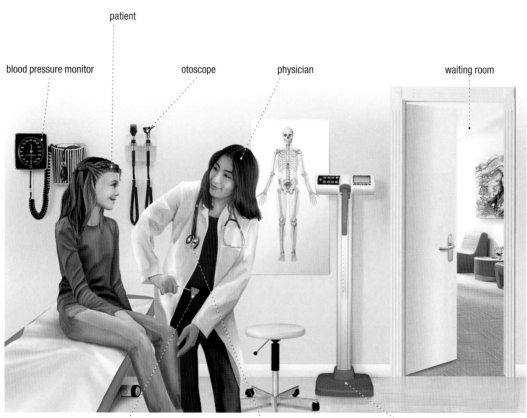

patient

blood pressure monitor   otoscope   physician   waiting room

reflex hammer   stethoscope   scale

bite	diabetes
frostbite	flu
inflammation	epilepsy
infection	asthma
nasal congestion	appointment
sore throat	examination
sneeze	symptom
nausea	diagnosis
vomiting	prescription
diarrhea	blood sample
constipation	to catch a cold
allergy	to be absent from school
food intolerance	to take medicine
back pain	to rest
stomachache	I need to see a doctor.
chickenpox	I feel sick.
mumps	It hurts here.
measles	I'm allergic to…

Body and Health

pharmacy

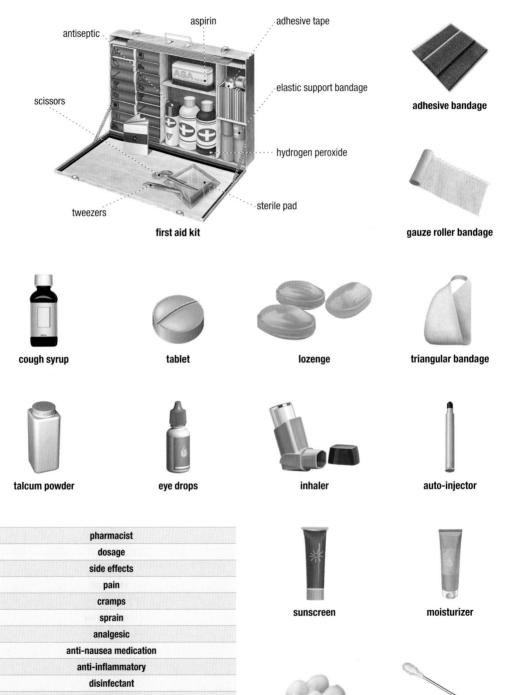

antiseptic

aspirin

adhesive tape

scissors

elastic support bandage

hydrogen peroxide

tweezers

sterile pad

first aid kit

adhesive bandage

gauze roller bandage

cough syrup

tablet

lozenge

triangular bandage

talcum powder

eye drops

inhaler

auto-injector

pharmacist
dosage
side effects
pain
cramps
sprain
analgesic
anti-nausea medication
anti-inflammatory
disinfectant
antihistamine
vitamin
insulin

sunscreen

moisturizer

absorbent cotton

cotton swab

hospital

patient room

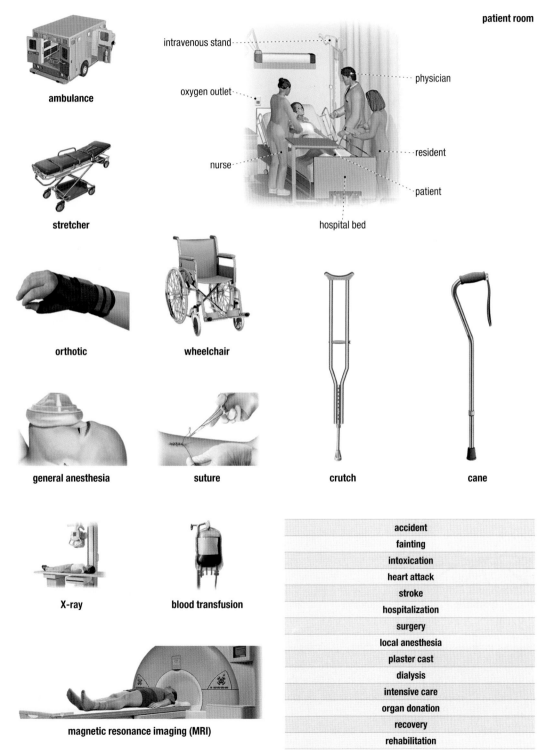

ambulance

intravenous stand

oxygen outlet

physician

nurse

resident

patient

stretcher

hospital bed

orthotic

wheelchair

general anesthesia

suture

crutch

cane

X-ray

blood transfusion

magnetic resonance imaging (MRI)

accident
fainting
intoxication
heart attack
stroke
hospitalization
surgery
local anesthesia
plaster cast
dialysis
intensive care
organ donation
recovery
rehabilitation

Body and Health

Body and Health

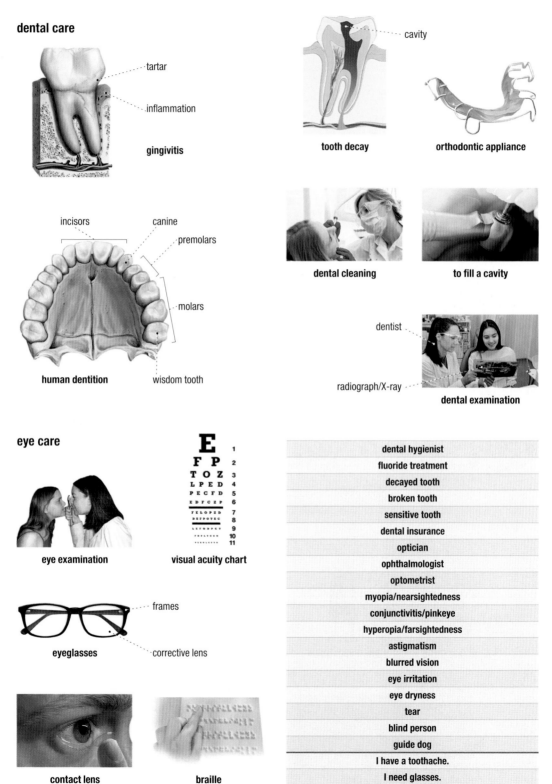

dental care

tartar

inflammation

gingivitis

cavity

tooth decay

orthodontic appliance

incisors

canine

premolars

molars

human dentition

wisdom tooth

dental cleaning

to fill a cavity

dentist

radiograph/X-ray

dental examination

eye care

eye examination

E
F P
T O Z
L P E D
P E C F D
E D F C Z P
F E L O P Z D
D E F P O T E C
L E F O D P C T
F P L T C E O
P E Z O L C F T D

1
2
3
4
5
6
7
8
9
10
11

visual acuity chart

frames

corrective lens

eyeglasses

contact lens

braille

dental hygienist
fluoride treatment
decayed tooth
broken tooth
sensitive tooth
dental insurance
optician
ophthalmologist
optometrist
myopia/nearsightedness
conjunctivitis/pinkeye
hyperopia/farsightedness
astigmatism
blurred vision
eye irritation
eye dryness
tear
blind person
guide dog
I have a toothache.
I need glasses.

Body and Health

ear care

hearing test

audiologist

hearing aid

hearing-impaired person

sign language

therapy

physical therapy   **acupuncture**

psychotherapy session   psychologist

massage therapy

massage

hydrotherapy

yoga

prevention

hearing loss
otitis/ear infection
deafness
tinnitus
traditional medicine
alternative medicine
mental health
chiropractic
sports medicine
light therapy
My ear hurts.
I have difficulty hearing.
I'm in therapy.

physical exercise

healthy diet

vaccination

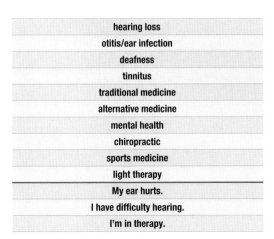

rest

The materials used to cover the building, the flat or peaked shape of the roof, the addition of a garage and the number of floors are all factors that help to determine the outside appearance of a house. The land surrounding a house is also an important element, whether it consists of a narrow flower bed or is large enough to house a swimming pool, vegetable garden and shed.

exterior of a house

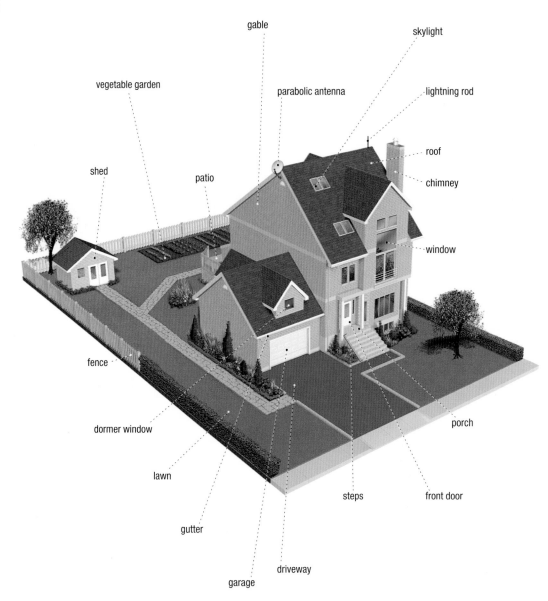

gable

skylight

vegetable garden

parabolic antenna

lightning rod

roof

shed

chimney

patio

window

fence

dormer window

porch

lawn

steps

front door

gutter

driveway

garage

city houses

high-rise apartment

one-story house

two-story house

duplex

town houses

condominiums

traditional houses

igloo

yurt

hut

adobe house

hut

isba

tepee

pile dwelling

owner	elevator
tenant	alarm system
rent	heating
key	air-conditioning
lock	thermostat
janitor	for sale
house number	for rent
mailbox	to live in town
intercom	to live in the suburbs
door bell	to live in the country

The rooms in a house are either all on one floor or spread over several floors. In our modern world, the number of rooms will vary from one house to another, depending on the family's needs and budgets. Any sizeable home will include a kitchen, dining room, living room, bathroom and at least one bedroom.

main rooms

Home

first floor

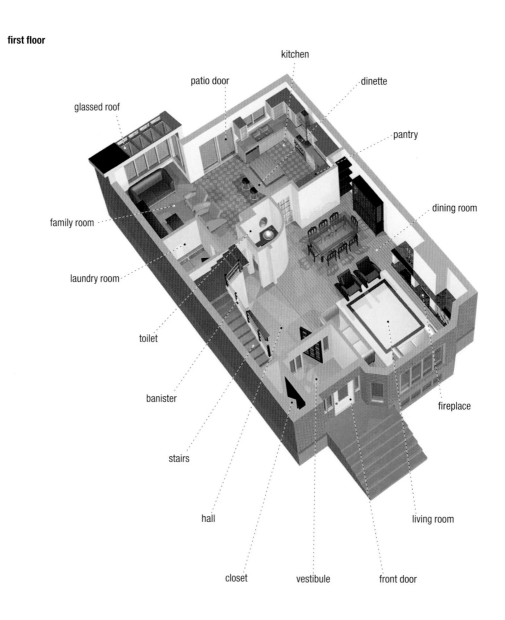

kitchen

patio door

dinette

glassed roof

pantry

family room

dining room

laundry room

toilet

banister

fireplace

stairs

hall

living room

closet   vestibule   front door

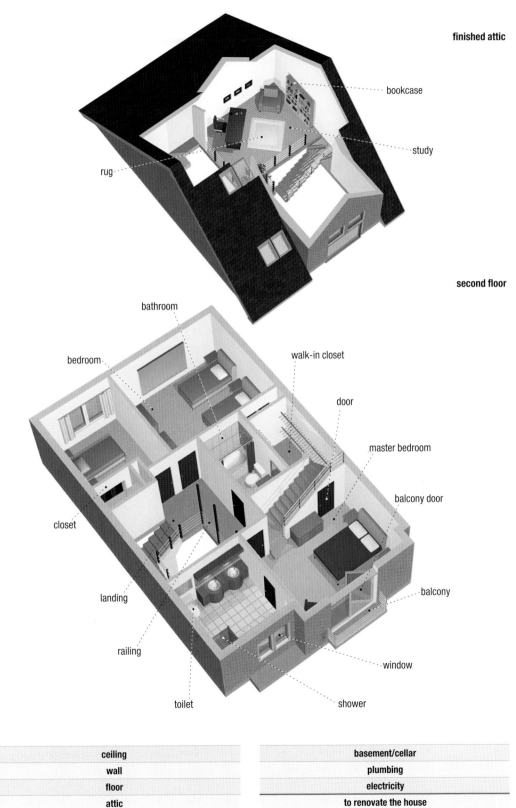

Home

finished attic

bookcase

study

rug

second floor

bathroom

bedroom

walk-in closet

door

master bedroom

closet

balcony door

landing

balcony

railing

window

toilet

shower

ceiling	basement/cellar
wall	plumbing
floor	electricity
attic	to renovate the house

Home

Bedrooms are for sleeping in. They can be decorated in all kinds of ways, depending on taste, but the bed is usually the main item of furniture. Next to it, closets, wardrobes or dressers are for storing clothes and other personal effects. Bedrooms are usually intimate and comfortable places. We go into them for rest, peace and quiet.

furnishings

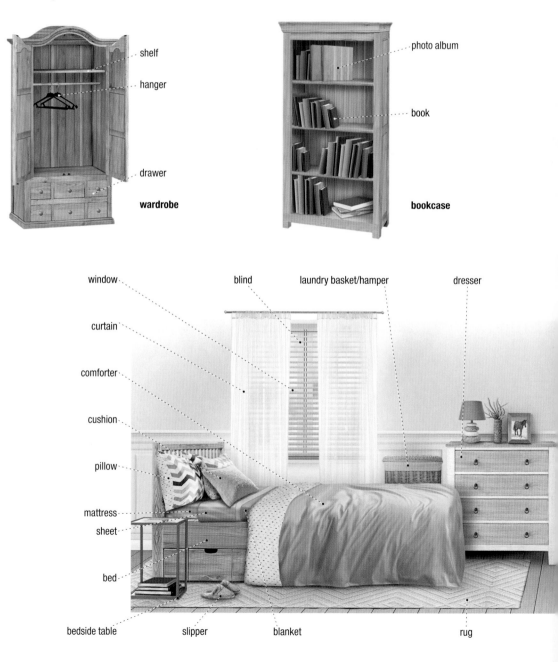

shelf

hanger

drawer

wardrobe

photo album

book

bookcase

window

curtain

comforter

cushion

pillow

mattress

sheet

bed

bedside table

blind

laundry basket/hamper

dresser

slipper

blanket

rug

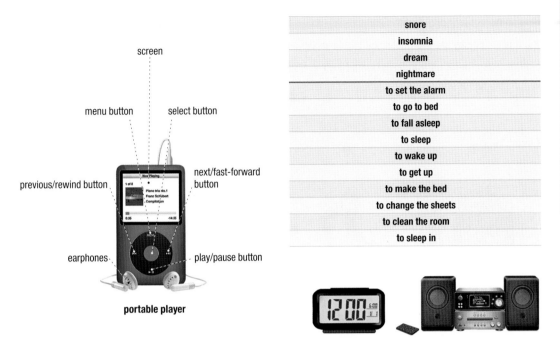

screen

menu button

select button

next/fast-forward button

previous/rewind button

earphones

play/pause button

Now Playing
1 of 8
Piano trio No.1
Franz Schubert
Compilation
0:35   -14:35

portable player

snore
insomnia
dream
nightmare
to set the alarm
to go to bed
to fall asleep
to sleep
to wake up
to get up
to make the bed
to change the sheets
to clean the room
to sleep in

12:00 6:00

alarm clock

mini stereo sound system

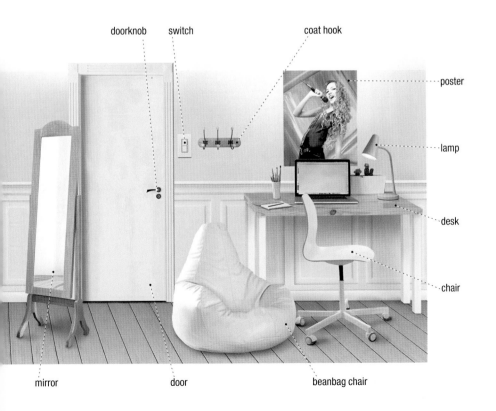

doorknob   switch

coat hook

poster

lamp

desk

chair

mirror   door

beanbag chair

Home

underwear and clothing

briefs

bra

sock

pajamas

boxer shorts

pantyhose/tights

shorts

camisole

pants

dress

skirt

T-shirt

button

fly

jeans

collar

pocket

sleeve

shirt

sweater

blouse

hood

zipper

coat

raincoat/anorak

jacket

91727

accessories and shoes

glove

mitten

watch

eyeglasses

scarf

necktie

belt

wallet

cap

stocking cap

jewelry

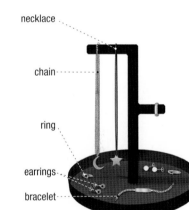

necklace

chain

ring

earrings

bracelet

head scarf

hat

umbrella

bag

boot

winter boot

shoelace

outsole

shoe

running shoe

sandal

Home

People have been taking baths since time immemorial, but it took until the 19th century for running water to appear in bathrooms. In today's homes, bathrooms often come with a toilet, sink, shower and bathtub. Bathrooms, whether they are large or small, plain or fancy, are places dedicated to hygiene.

bar soap   **shampoo**   **conditioner**   **washcloth**

bathroom

washcloth

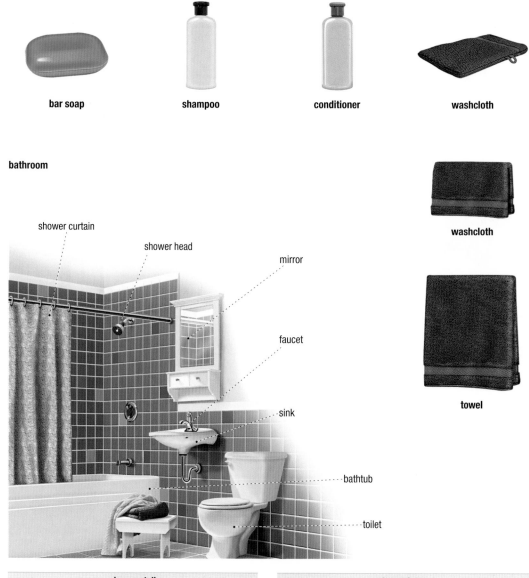

towel

shower stall	to wash up
bath mat	to take a shower
medicine cabinet	to take a bath
hand soap	to brush teeth
shower gel	to do hair
to use the bathroom	to put on makeup
to flush	to shave

body care

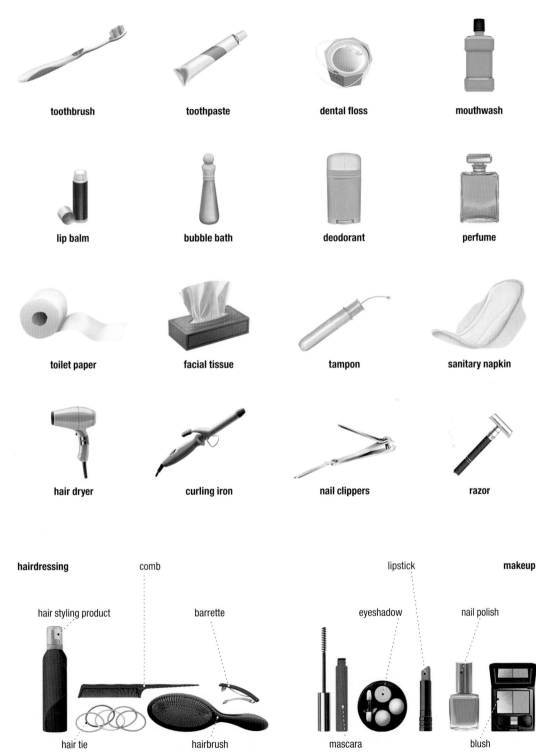

toothbrush

toothpaste

dental floss

mouthwash

lip balm

bubble bath

deodorant

perfume

toilet paper

facial tissue

tampon

sanitary napkin

hair dryer

curling iron

nail clippers

razor

hairdressing   comb   lipstick   **makeup**

hair styling product   barrette   eyeshadow   nail polish

hair tie   hairbrush   mascara   blush

Living rooms, playrooms, and dining rooms are valuable rooms in a house. That is where the family gathers to share a meal, watch TV, use communication devices or play games, singly or in groups.

games

checkers

chess

die

playing piece

board game

playing cards

dominoes

jigsaw puzzle

blocks

living room

floor lamp

armchair

fan

cushion

sofa

table lamp

coffee table

living room

futon	to sit down in the living room
team	to watch television
winner	to receive guests
loser	to serve the meal
breakfast	to set/clear the table
lunch	Let's play a game.
dinner	It's time to eat.

Home

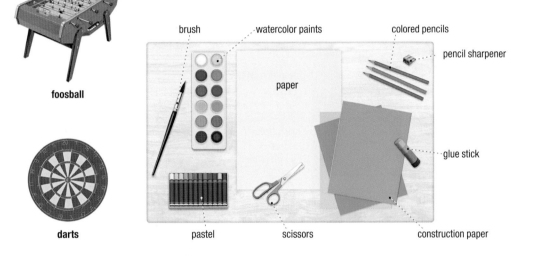

foosball

brush   watercolor paints   colored pencils   pencil sharpener

paper

glue stick

darts   pastel   scissors   construction paper

dining room

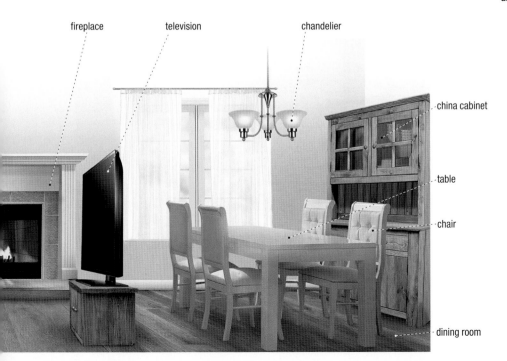

fireplace   television   chandelier   china cabinet

table

chair

dining room

Along with TV and radio, the telephone remains one of the most important forms of telecommunication. The technology for all those devices keeps getting better. The Internet, a vast international communications system, provides more and more options and is revolutionizing the media world by connecting millions of people, organizations and businesses.

Home

smartphone

receiver

objective lens

camera

sound/silent switch

sleep/wake button

09:50

USB port

volume buttons

touch screen

home button

headphone jack

speaker

microphone

mobile phone

receiver

display

end call key

menu key

camera key

call keys

navigation key

keyboard

microphone

docking station

cordless telephone　　　　**digital answering machine**　　　　**portable earphone**　　　　**adapter**

tablet computer

sleep/wake button

volume buttons

09:50

touch screen

home button

earbuds

digital book reader

wireless headphones

portable player

stylus

portable game console

portable DVD player

wireless speaker

smart watch

display

game console

video entertainment system

controller

compact disc player

USB port

loudspeaker

mini stereo sound system

voice mail
ringing
wrong number
to make a call
to answer
to hang up
to hear/leave a message
to send/receive a text message (SMS)
to listen to music
to play video games

remote control

television set

digital video recorder/ receiver

Home

Internet network

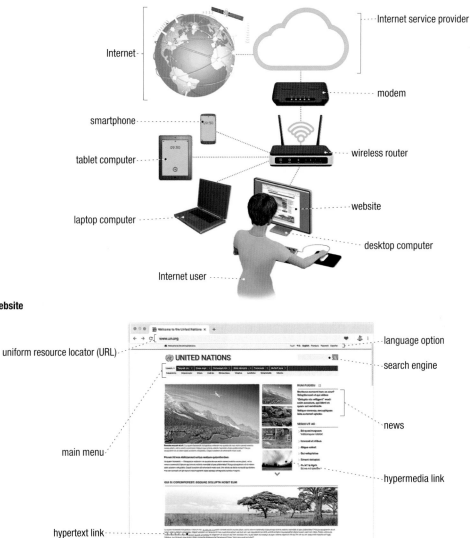

- Internet
- Internet service provider
- modem
- smartphone
- tablet computer
- wireless router
- website
- laptop computer
- desktop computer
- Internet user

website

- uniform resource locator (URL)
- language option
- search engine
- main menu
- news
- hypermedia link
- hypertext link

UNITED NATIONS

www.un.org

online	to send as an attachment
offline	to bookmark
reply	to send a message/document
spam	to download a file
email address	to forward
wireless Internet access (Wi-Fi)	to subscribe
fake news	to unsubscribe
cyberbullying	to have/open an account
hacking	to log in/log on
to select	to log out/log off
to browse	

Internet uses

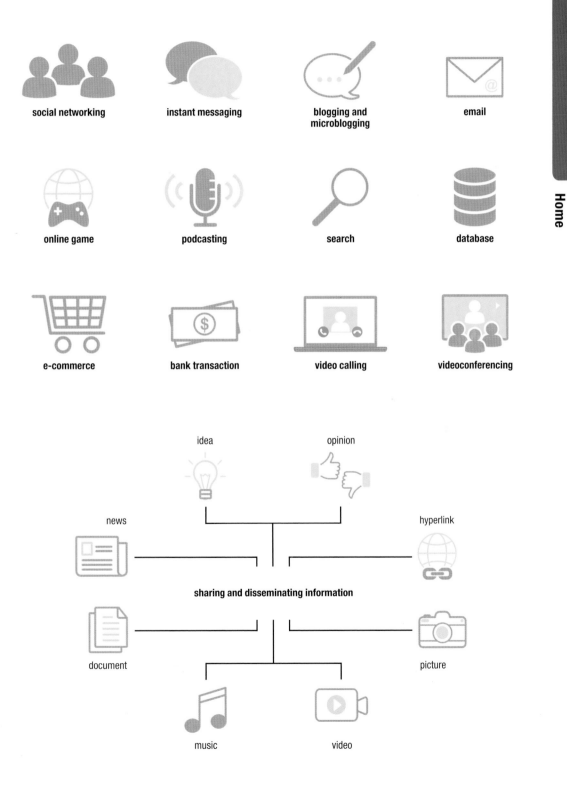

social networking

instant messaging

blogging and
microblogging

email

online game

podcasting

search

database

e-commerce

bank transaction

video calling

videoconferencing

idea

opinion

news

hyperlink

sharing and disseminating information

document

picture

music

video

Home

The kitchen is where food is prepared and stored. It may or may not have a small dining area. Today's kitchens come with a refrigerator, stove and a whole range of small appliances and utensils. Cooks have a variety of tools at their disposal to help them prepare and cook food quickly and efficiently.

kitchen

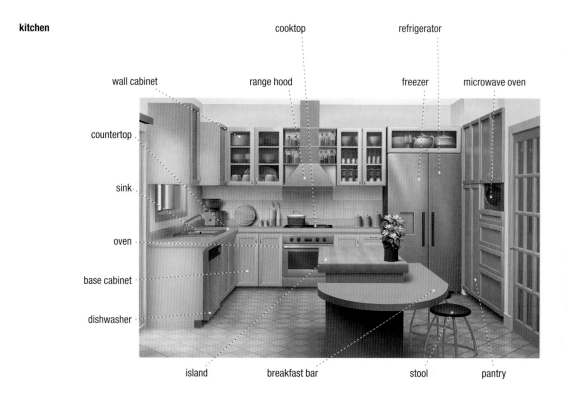

cooktop · refrigerator · wall cabinet · range hood · freezer · microwave oven · countertop · sink · oven · base cabinet · dishwasher · island · breakfast bar · stool · pantry

tableware

knife · soup bowl · glass · spoon · fork · cup · pepper mill · tablecloth · table napkin · plate · salt shaker

kitchen equipment

kitchen utensils

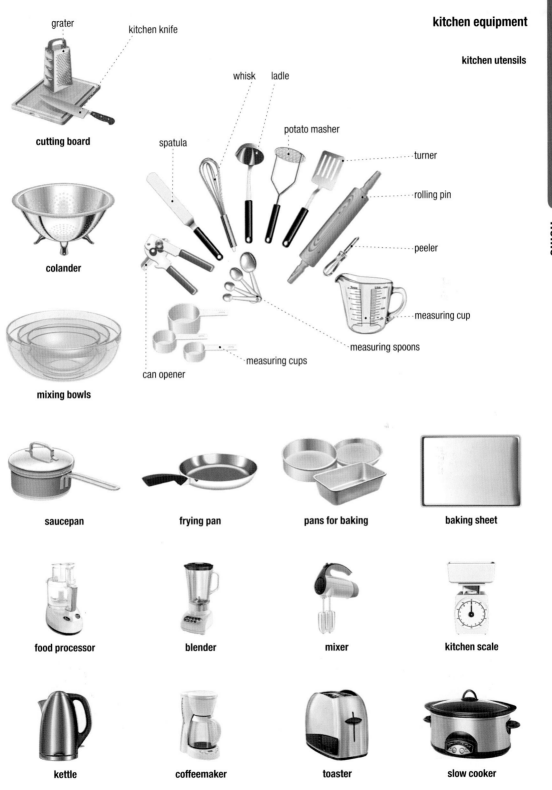

grater

kitchen knife

whisk   ladle

potato masher

turner

rolling pin

spatula

cutting board

peeler

colander

measuring cup

measuring spoons

can opener

measuring cups

mixing bowls

saucepan

frying pan

pans for baking

baking sheet

food processor

blender

mixer

kitchen scale

kettle

coffeemaker

toaster

slow cooker

Meals are made up of foods that vary according to the time of the day and the part of the world in which they are eaten. Most food falls into broad categories like fruits, vegetables or cereal products. Each type of food supplies our bodies with different nutritional elements (proteins, carbohydrates, vitamins, minerals, etc.).

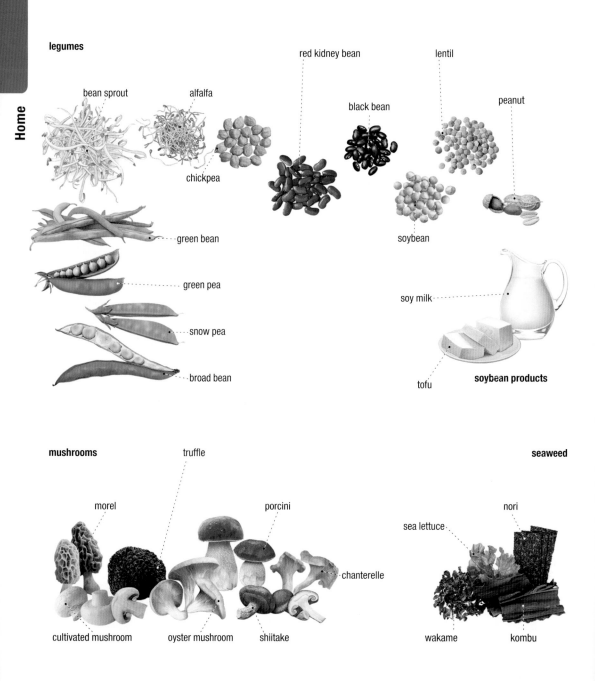

legumes

bean sprout

alfalfa

red kidney bean

lentil

black bean

peanut

chickpea

green bean

soybean

green pea

soy milk

snow pea

broad bean

tofu

soybean products

mushrooms

truffle

seaweed

morel

porcini

nori

sea lettuce

chanterelle

cultivated mushroom

oyster mushroom

shiitake

wakame

kombu

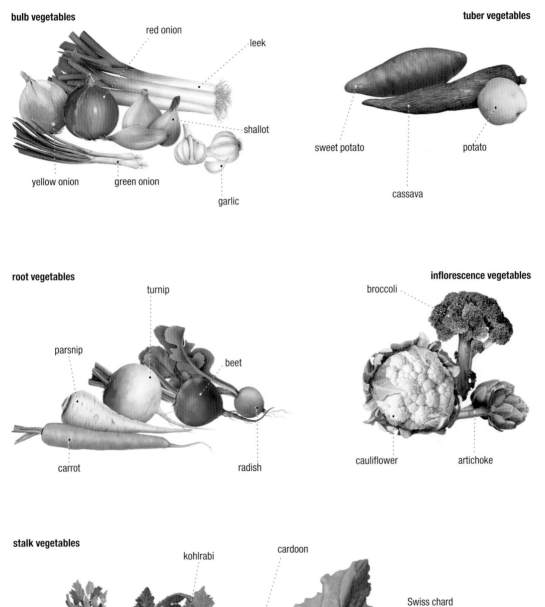

bulb vegetables

red onion

leek

shallot

yellow onion

green onion

garlic

tuber vegetables

sweet potato

potato

cassava

root vegetables

turnip

parsnip

beet

carrot

radish

inflorescence vegetables

broccoli

cauliflower

artichoke

stalk vegetables

kohlrabi

cardoon

Swiss chard

asparagus

celery

rhubarb

fennel

Home

leaf vegetables

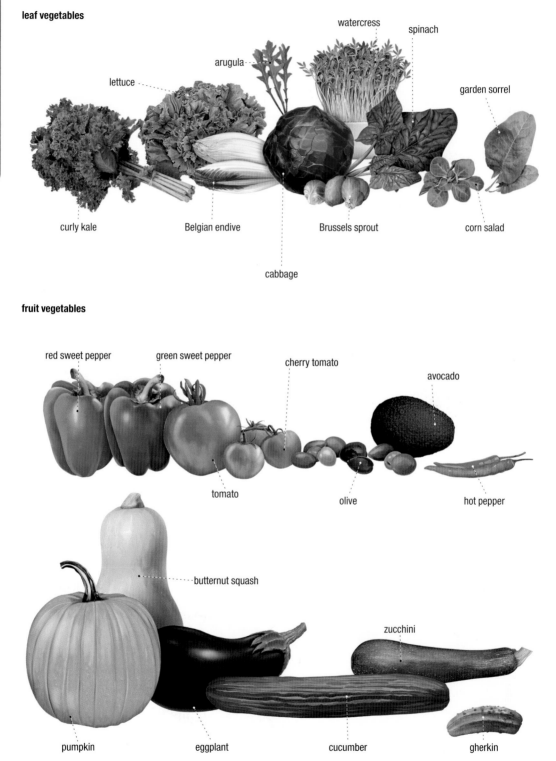

watercress
spinach
arugula
lettuce
garden sorrel

curly kale
Belgian endive
Brussels sprout
corn salad

cabbage

fruit vegetables

red sweet pepper
green sweet pepper
cherry tomato
avocado

tomato
olive
hot pepper

butternut squash

zucchini

pumpkin
eggplant
cucumber
gherkin

pome fruits

berries

strawberry   blackberry

cranberry

pear

grape

blueberry

apple

currant

bilberry

raspberry

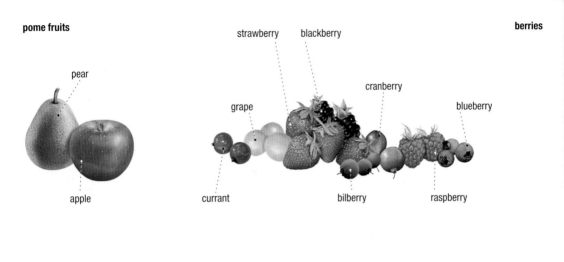

stone fruits   peach

citrus fruits

grapefruit

plum

nectarine

lemon

clementine

cherry

apricot

date

lime   orange

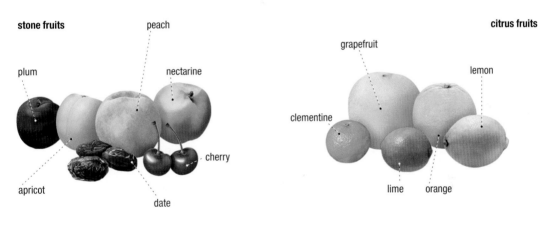

melons

tropical fruits

pineapple

honeydew melon

papaya

pomegranate

mango

watermelon

banana

kiwi   fig   passion fruit

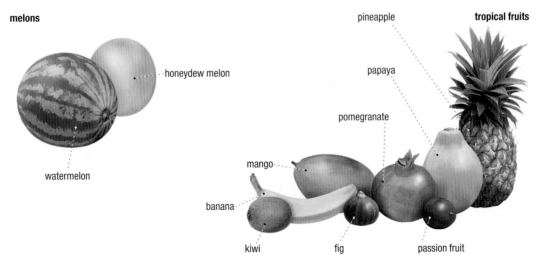

seeds

nuts

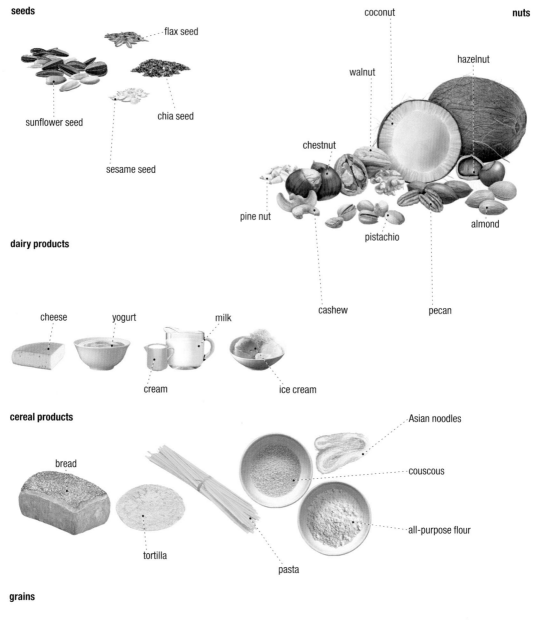

- flax seed
- sunflower seed
- chia seed
- sesame seed

- coconut
- walnut
- hazelnut
- chestnut
- pine nut
- pistachio
- almond
- cashew
- pecan

dairy products

- cheese
- yogurt
- milk
- cream
- ice cream

cereal products

- Asian noodles
- couscous
- bread
- all-purpose flour
- tortilla
- pasta

grains

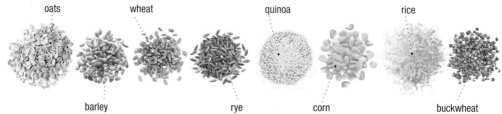

- oats
- wheat
- quinoa
- rice
- barley
- rye
- corn
- buckwheat

Home

mollusks

oyster

mussel

squid

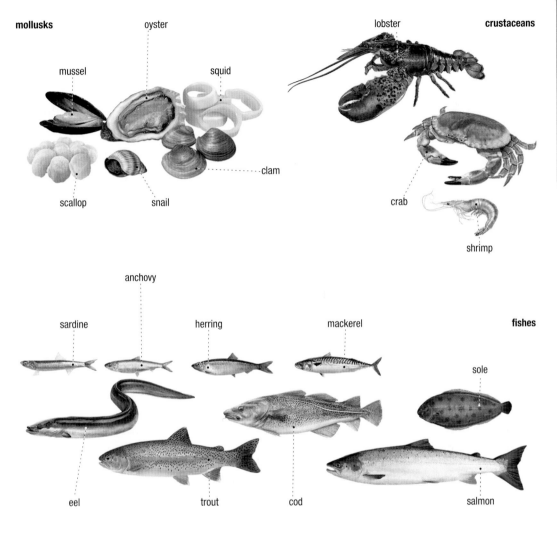

clam

scallop

snail

crustaceans

lobster

crab

shrimp

fishes

anchovy

sardine

herring

mackerel

sole

eel

trout

cod

salmon

meats

lamb

beef

veal

ham

sausage

pork

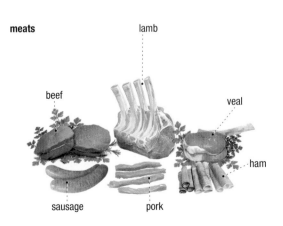

poultry

turkey

duck

chicken

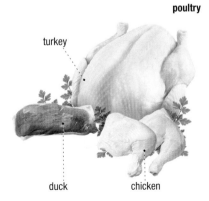

Home

herbs

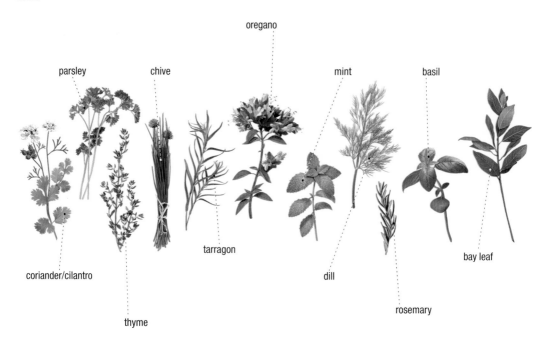

parsley

chive

oregano

mint

basil

coriander/cilantro

tarragon

dill

bay leaf

thyme

rosemary

spices

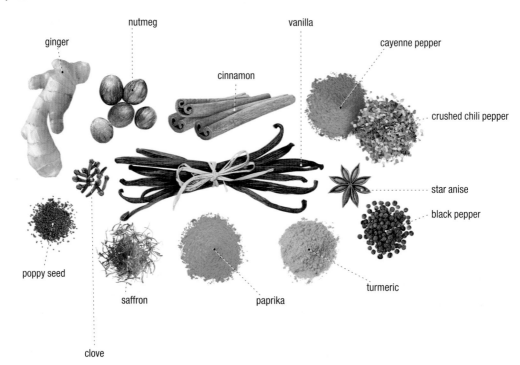

ginger

nutmeg

vanilla

cayenne pepper

cinnamon

crushed chili pepper

star anise

black pepper

poppy seed

saffron

paprika

turmeric

clove

condiments and cooking ingredients

oil

white vinegar

balsamic vinegar

table salt

mustard

mayonnaise

ketchup

relish

capers

horseradish

hot sauce

soy sauce

hummus

butter

margarine

sugar

brown sugar

honey

molasses

maple syrup

cocoa

carob

baking powder

baking soda

Home

cooking techniques

to cut

to peel

to rinse

to pour

to grate

to grind

to mix

to whip

to cook

to refrigerate

to freeze

to thaw/defrost

special diets

gluten-free

lactose-free

egg-free

no added sugar

salt-free

trans-fat free

meat free

vegetarian/vegan

cooking methods

to boil

to fry/pan fry

to grill

to roast

steam cooking

slow cooking

high heat cooking

low heat cooking

containers and wraps

containers

bottle

can

bag

mason jar

drink can

plastic container

wraps

aluminum foil

plastic wrap

parchment paper

waxed paper

healthy diet	to simmer
intolerance/allergy	to serve
apron	to season
oven mitt	to reheat a dish
paper towel	I like…
to cook	I don't like…
to preheat the oven	I'm allergic to…

Home

everyday dishes

soup

sandwich

salad dressing

salad

bread

pasta

pizza

hamburger

french fries

sauce

fried chicken

steak

stew

rice

pie

curry

omelet

kabob

breakfast

cracker

orange juice

toast

pastries

cereal/muesli

fruit yogurt

jam

butter

egg

fresh fruit

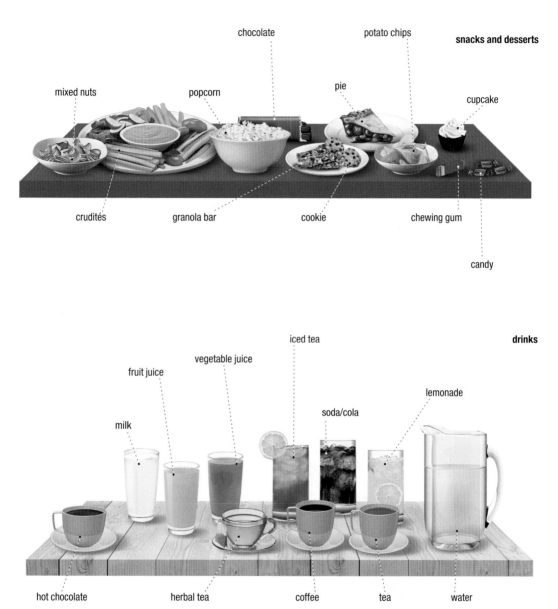

snacks and desserts

mixed nuts

chocolate

potato chips

popcorn

pie

cupcake

crudités

granola bar

cookie

chewing gum

candy

drinks

milk

fruit juice

vegetable juice

iced tea

soda/cola

lemonade

hot chocolate

herbal tea

coffee

tea

water

raw/cooked food	to have a meal
small/large portion	to eat
prepared meal	to drink
delivery service	to invite
mealtime	to share
light meal	I'm hungry!
hearty meal	Enjoy your meal!
balanced meal	It's delicious!

Home

Until electricity was invented, household tasks relied on muscle power. Electric motors are now used to operate appliances and tools like clothes washers or electric drills that make household work easier. Many household tools that don't require electricity are still in use.

household equipment

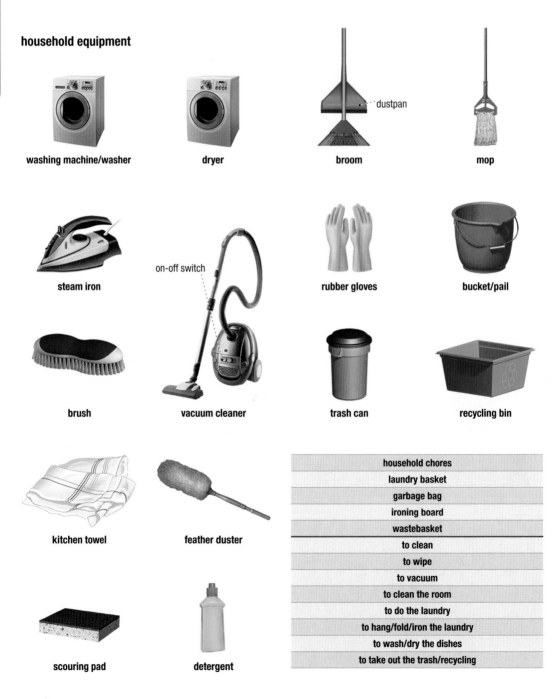

washing machine/washer

dryer

dustpan

broom

mop

steam iron

on-off switch

rubber gloves

bucket/pail

brush

vacuum cleaner

trash can

recycling bin

kitchen towel

feather duster

scouring pad

detergent

household chores
laundry basket
garbage bag
ironing board
wastebasket
to clean
to wipe
to vacuum
to clean the room
to do the laundry
to hang/fold/iron the laundry
to wash/dry the dishes
to take out the trash/recycling

home maintenance and repairs

pliers

toolbox

tape measure

level

crescent wrench

screw

nail

screwdriver

hammer

saw

drill/driver

stepladder

tray

paint roller

painting material

brush

pet care

aquarium

birdcage

pet carrier

litter box

bowl   water dispenser

tag

small animal cage

bowl

collar

leash

Home

Whether cultivating an ornamental garden, growing a vegetable plot or arranging a small flower box, gardening is a popular pastime. Gardens vary in appearance according to the gardener's taste, the space available and local conditions. You will get the most out of your plot if you learn about plants suitable for your region and choose the best tools.

Home

garden

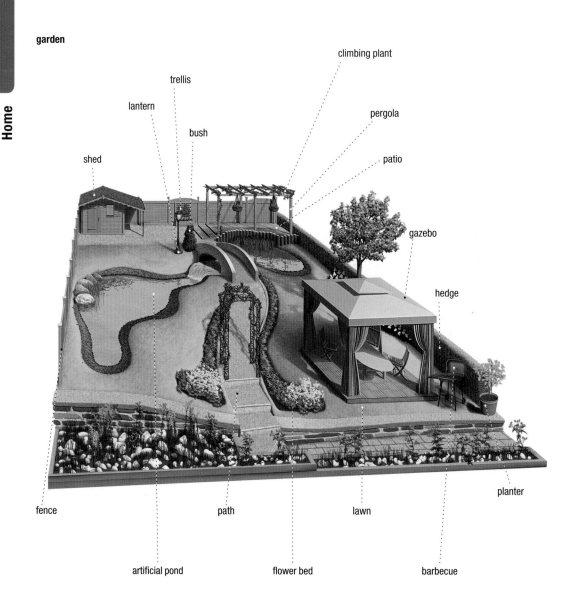

climbing plant

trellis

lantern

pergola

bush

patio

shed

gazebo

hedge

fence

path

lawn

planter

artificial pond

flower bed

barbecue

Home

gardening material

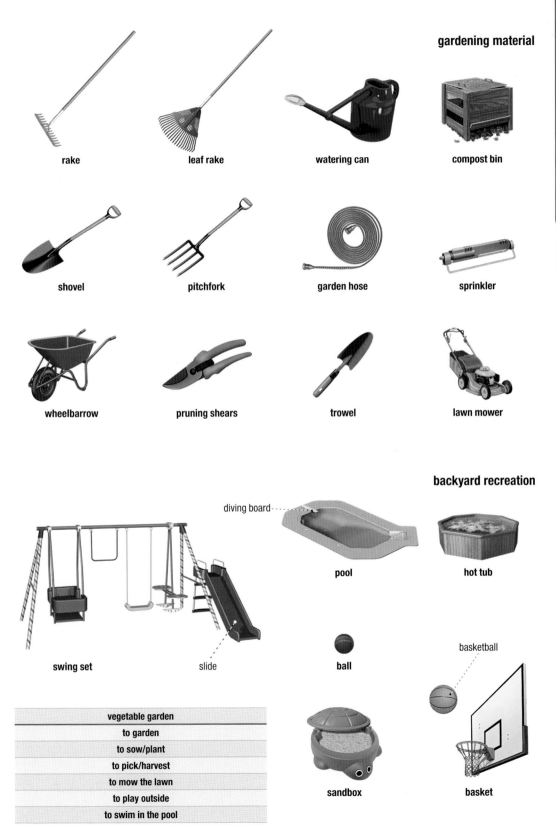

rake

leaf rake

watering can

compost bin

shovel

pitchfork

garden hose

sprinkler

wheelbarrow

pruning shears

trowel

lawn mower

backyard recreation

diving board

pool

hot tub

swing set

slide

ball

basketball

sandbox

basket

| vegetable garden |
| to garden |
| to sow/plant |
| to pick/harvest |
| to mow the lawn |
| to play outside |
| to swim in the pool |

Transportation

The invention of the wheel enabled humans to travel farther and faster, eventually leading to the creation of bicycles, motorcycles and automobiles. Since motorized vehicles first made their appearance in the 19th century, they have not stopped evolving and gaining in popularity. Because of the large numbers of cars on the road, people are now being encouraged to increase their use of public transportation (buses, trains) and ride their bikes when possible to reduce traffic congestion and air pollution.

cycling transport

bicycle/bike

bike rental
bike repair
bicycle parking
city bicycle
mountain bike
safety vest
bicycle bell
kickstand
inner tube
to ride a bicycle
to brake
to shift gears
to inflate a tire
to fix a flat tire

helmet   **lock**

tool kit   **bicycle bag**

school bus flashing lights

bus baggage compartment

bus ticket **stop button**

public transportation/public transit

bus station
ticket counter
ticket machine
one-way ticket
round-trip ticket
departure time
arrival time
travel time
route
destination
pass
student rate
priority seat
to wait for the bus
to take the bus
to get on the bus
to get off the bus
Does this bus go to…
Which bus goes to…
I would like a ticket for…
I missed my bus.
Can you tell me when we get to…

Transportation

city bus

bus stop bus shelter route sign

schedule passenger door driver

Transportation

automotive transport

motorcycle

handgrip   mirror

front turn signal

gas tank

seat

headlight

taillight

face shield

rear turn signal

engine

motorcycle helmet

touring motorcycle   moped   motor scooter   off-road motorcycle

micro compact car   hatchback   four-door hatchback   four-door sedan

sports car   convertible   station wagon   minivan

new car	air-conditioning system
used car	to fasten the seat belt
hybrid car	to open/close the window
electric car	to lock the doors
car sharing service	to unlock the doors
radio	to put on music
ride-sharing service	to take a taxi

automotive transport

motor home

minibus

limousine

taxi

all-terrain vehicle (ATV)

off-road vehicle

sport-utility vehicle (SUV)

pickup truck

box van

semitrailer

truck tractor

tow truck

dump truck

garbage truck

tank truck

cement mixer

grader

street sweeper

snowblower

truck crane

blade

bulldozer

backhoe loader

Transportation

service station

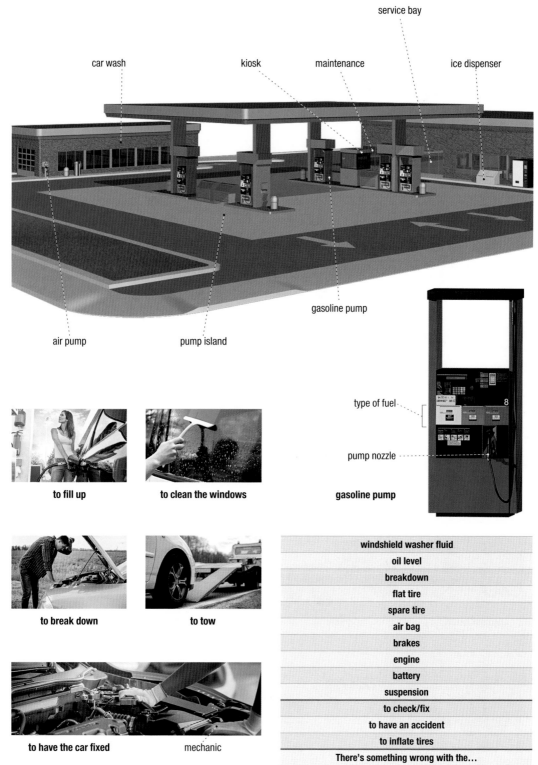

service bay

car wash   kiosk   maintenance   ice dispenser

gasoline pump

air pump   pump island

type of fuel

8

pump nozzle

to fill up   **to clean the windows**   **gasoline pump**

to break down   **to tow**

windshield washer fluid
oil level
breakdown
flat tire
spare tire
air bag
brakes
engine
battery
suspension
to check/fix
to have an accident
to inflate tires
There's something wrong with the...

to have the car fixed   mechanic

Transportation

road map legends

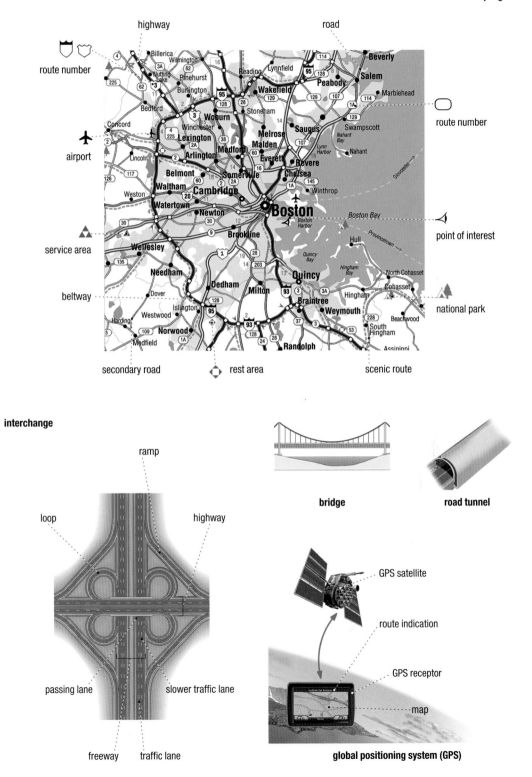

highway

road

route number

route number

airport

point of interest

service area

national park

beltway

secondary road

rest area

scenic route

interchange

ramp

loop

highway

passing lane

slower traffic lane

freeway

traffic lane

bridge

road tunnel

GPS satellite

route indication

GPS receptor

map

global positioning system (GPS)

traffic signs

stop at intersection

merging traffic/priority intersection

yield

reverse turn/double bend

right curve/right bend

direction to be followed

two-way traffic

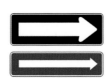

one-way traffic

traffic lights ahead

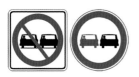

passing prohibited

no U-turn

railroad crossing/grade crossing

traffic circle/rotary

to start
to drive
to stop at a traffic light
to turn right/left
to continue straight ahead
to park
to pass

Transportation

traffic signs

road narrows

slippery road

bumps

falling rocks

steep hill

wildlife crossing

roadwork ahead

school zone

pedestrian crossing

no entry

closed to bicycles

closed to pedestrians

driving lesson
driver's license
license plate/number
no parking
speeding
ticket
demerit point

overhead clearance

Boats are among the oldest forms of transportation. By the 14th century, trade opportunities spurred the building of swift sailboats. Huge steam-powered passenger ships were all the rage in the 19th century. These days, waterways are mainly used for transporting goods at low cost.

Transportation

cruise ship

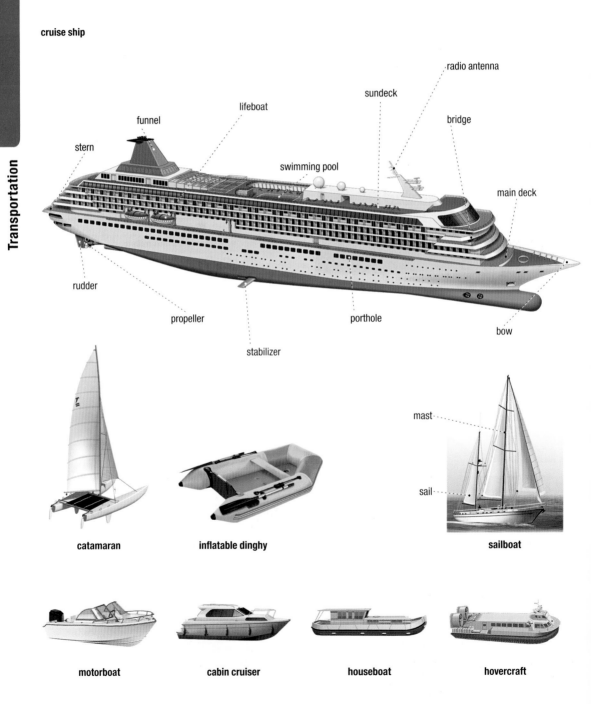

radio antenna

sundeck

lifeboat

bridge

funnel

stern

swimming pool

main deck

rudder

propeller

porthole

bow

stabilizer

catamaran

inflatable dinghy

mast

sail

sailboat

motorboat

cabin cruiser

houseboat

hovercraft

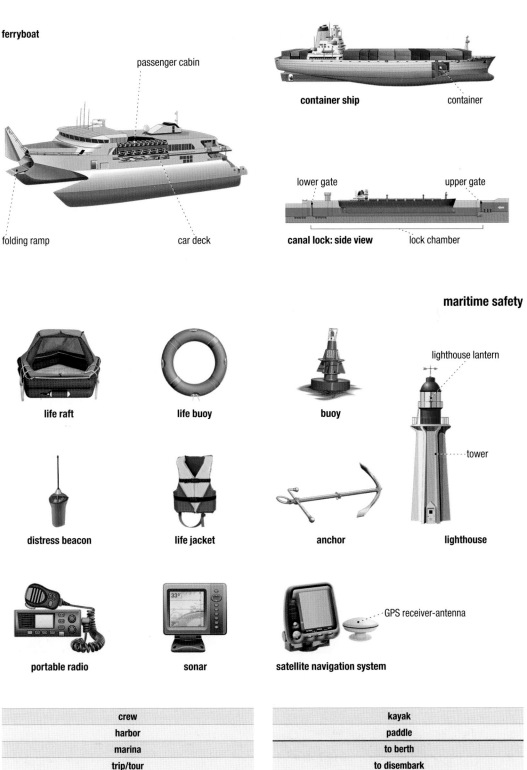

ferryboat

passenger cabin

folding ramp

car deck

container ship

container

lower gate

upper gate

canal lock: side view

lock chamber

maritime safety

life raft

life buoy

buoy

lighthouse lantern

tower

distress beacon

life jacket

anchor

lighthouse

portable radio

sonar

satellite navigation system

GPS receiver-antenna

crew	kayak
harbor	paddle
marina	to berth
trip/tour	to disembark
cruise	to weigh anchor
seasickness	to cast anchor
canoe	to board

Transportation

Hot-air balloons were the first aircraft, and came into use as early as the 18th century. Planes revolutionized the history of air travel; the first controlled flight took place in 1903. Since the 1950s, jet planes have been transporting more and more passengers on longer and longer flights. Helicopters, which can lift off vertically, make rescue operations easier.

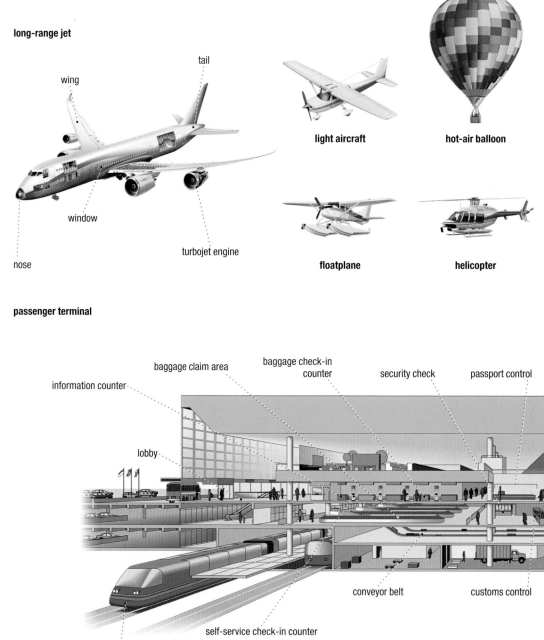

long-range jet

wing

tail

window

nose

turbojet engine

light aircraft

hot-air balloon

floatplane

helicopter

passenger terminal

information counter

baggage claim area

baggage check-in counter

security check

passport control

lobby

railroad shuttle service

self-service check-in counter

conveyor belt

customs control

Transportation

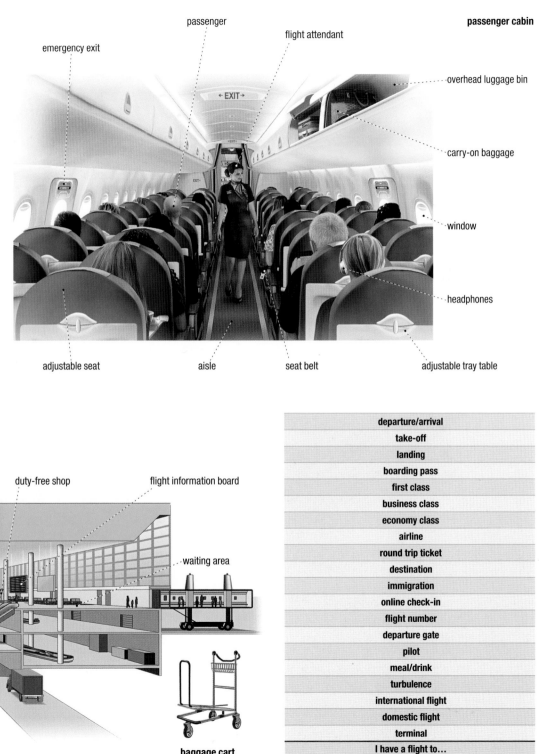

passenger

flight attendant

passenger cabin

emergency exit

overhead luggage bin

← EXIT →

carry-on baggage

window

headphones

adjustable seat

aisle

seat belt

adjustable tray table

duty-free shop

flight information board

waiting area

baggage cart

departure/arrival
take-off
landing
boarding pass
first class
business class
economy class
airline
round trip ticket
destination
immigration
online check-in
flight number
departure gate
pilot
meal/drink
turbulence
international flight
domestic flight
terminal
I have a flight to…

Cities are built-up areas that bring together a large number of people. Most of them live in residential neighborhoods and work downtown. The downtown area also houses the business core and establishments that offer a variety of goods and services. These establishments include libraries, museums, theaters and more.

City

downtown

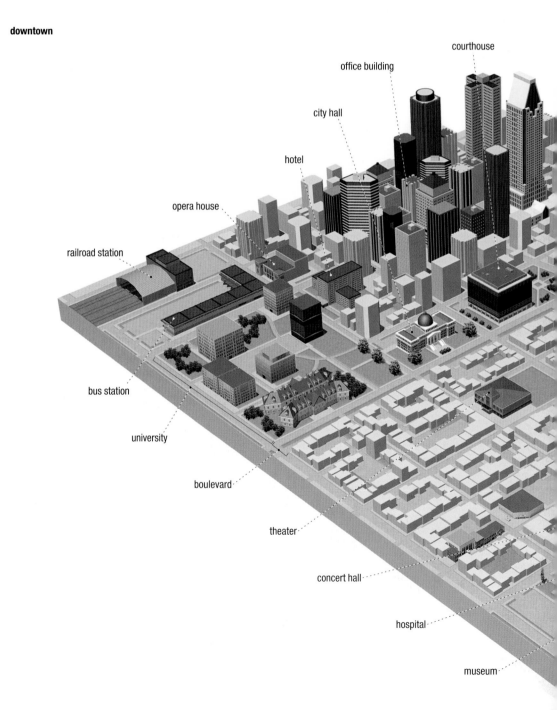

courthouse

office building

city hall

hotel

opera house

railroad station

bus station

university

boulevard

theater

concert hall

hospital

museum

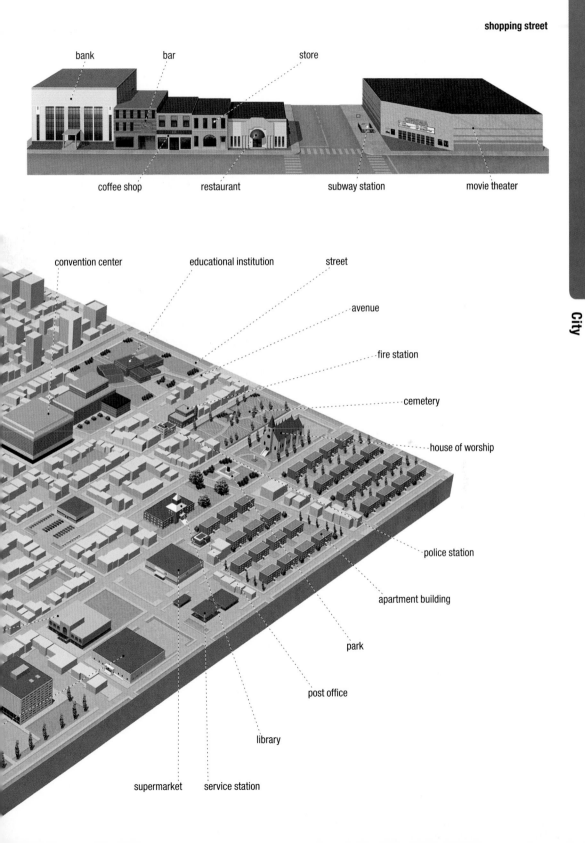

shopping street

bank

bar

store

coffee shop

restaurant

subway station

movie theater

City

convention center

educational institution

street

avenue

fire station

cemetery

house of worship

police station

apartment building

park

post office

library

supermarket

service station

City

urban map legends

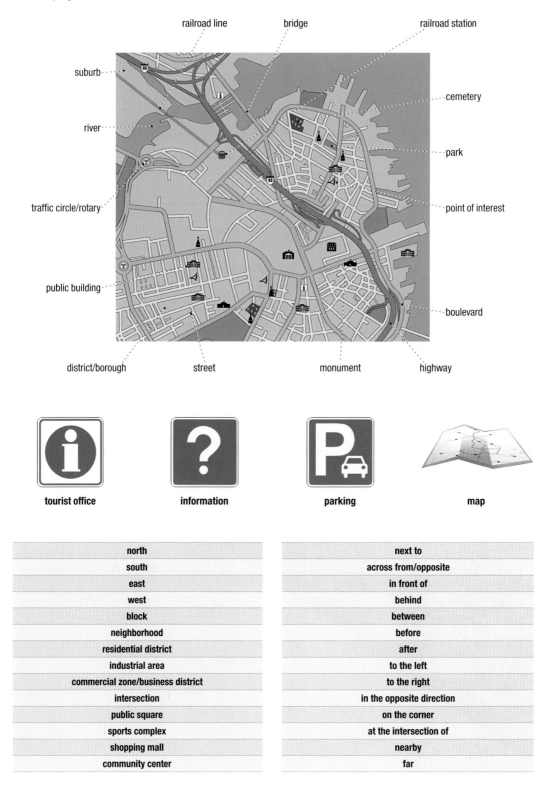

railroad line · bridge · railroad station

suburb

cemetery

river

park

traffic circle/rotary

point of interest

public building

boulevard

district/borough · street · monument · highway

tourist office · **information** · **parking** · **map**

north	next to
south	across from/opposite
east	in front of
west	behind
block	between
neighborhood	before
residential district	after
industrial area	to the left
commercial zone/business district	to the right
intersection	in the opposite direction
public square	on the corner
sports complex	at the intersection of
shopping mall	nearby
community center	far

street

City

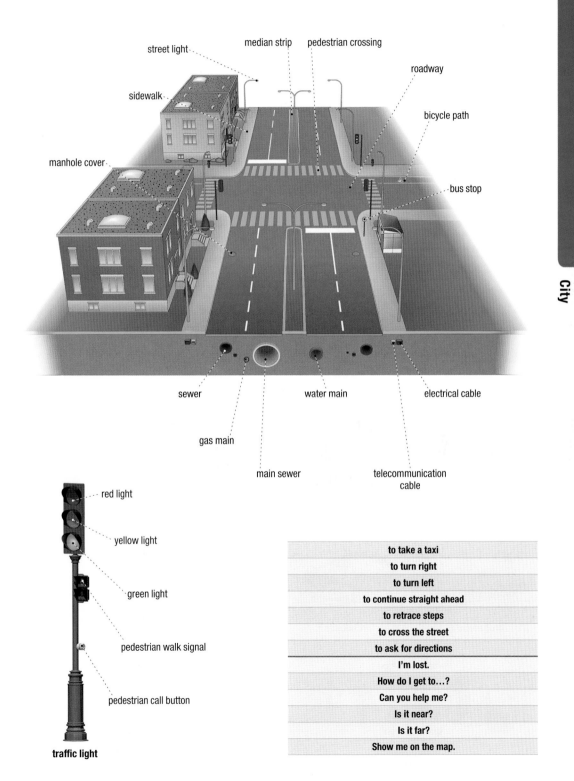

street light

median strip   pedestrian crossing

roadway

sidewalk

bicycle path

manhole cover

bus stop

sewer   water main   electrical cable

gas main

main sewer   telecommunication
cable

red light

yellow light

green light

pedestrian walk signal

pedestrian call button

traffic light

to take a taxi
to turn right
to turn left
to continue straight ahead
to retrace steps
to cross the street
to ask for directions
I'm lost.
How do I get to…?
Can you help me?
Is it near?
Is it far?
Show me on the map.

City

Emergency services are on hand to ensure our safety. The police are there to keep order, prevent crimes and help us when we need assistance. Firefighters put out fires and save lives. They are among the first on the scene, regardless of the danger.

police service

badge

pistol

burglary

theft

vandalism

graffiti

police car

police officer

crime scene tape

courtroom

crowd security

computer hacking

drug abuse

handcuffs

fingerprints

attack/assault
self-defense
investigator
missing person
suspect
arrest
lawyer
judge
guilty man/woman
innocent man/woman
to lodge a complaint
I was assaulted!
Someone stole my...
Help!
Thief!

fire prevention

fire truck

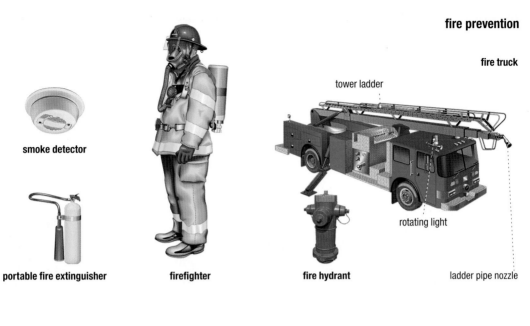

smoke detector

portable fire extinguisher

firefighter

tower ladder

rotating light

fire hydrant

ladder pipe nozzle

first aid

first aid supplies

oxygen cylinder

stretcher

ambulance

oxygen mask

cervical collar

fire
emergency exit
fall
minor/serious injury
breathing difficulty
breathing failure
immobilization
resuscitation
to take the pulse
to provide first aid
Fire!
Call emergency services!
I'm injured, help me!

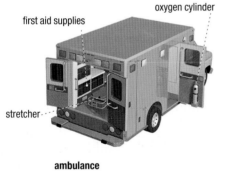

emergency medical technician (EMT)

witness

accident

victim

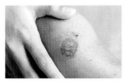

injury

material damage

City

All cities have public and commercial establishments offering all kinds of services: post offices, banks, libraries, stores, supermarkets, restaurants, hairdresser and more. They provide specialized goods and services like food, clothing, books, ready-made meals and other amenities.

mail

postal service network

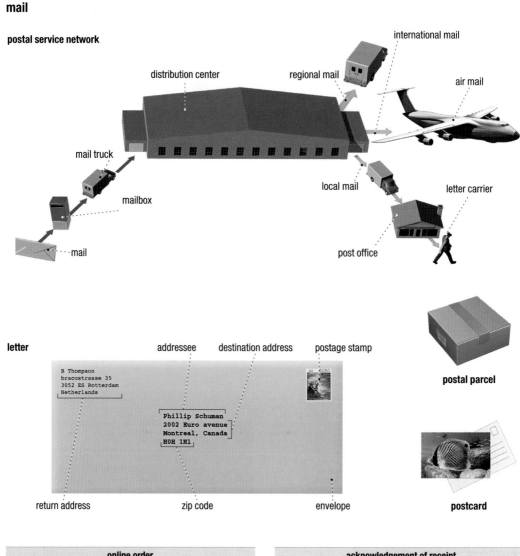

international mail

distribution center

regional mail

air mail

mail truck

local mail

letter carrier

mailbox

mail

post office

letter

addressee   destination address   postage stamp

B Thompson
bracostrasse 35
3052 ES Rotterdam
Netherlands

Phillip Schuman
2002 Euro avenue
Montreal, Canada
H0H 1H1

postal parcel

return address   zip code   envelope   **postcard**

online order	acknowledgement of receipt
shipping fees	signature
post office box (PO box)	to address an envelope
apartment number	to mail a letter
special delivery	to send a package
sender	to receive mail/a package
registered mail	Do not bend. Fragile!

bank and methods of payment

automated teller machine (ATM)

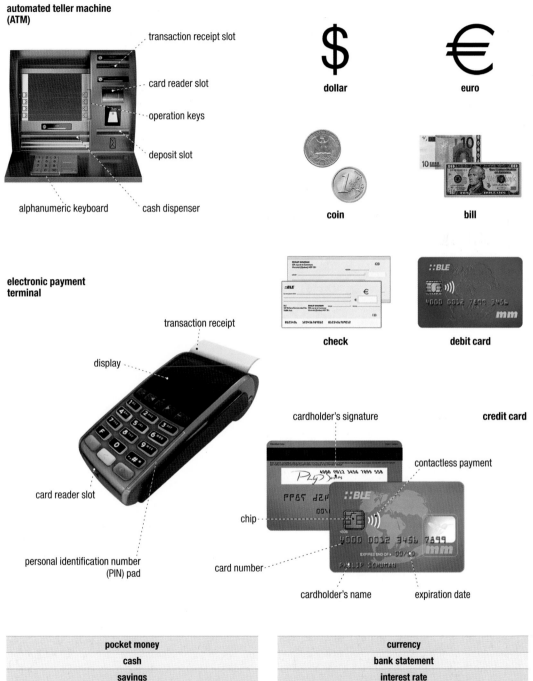

transaction receipt slot

card reader slot

operation keys

deposit slot

alphanumeric keyboard

cash dispenser

$

dollar

€

euro

coin

bill

City

electronic payment terminal

transaction receipt

display

card reader slot

personal identification number (PIN) pad

check

debit card

cardholder's signature

credit card

contactless payment

chip

card number

cardholder's name

expiration date

pocket money	currency
cash	bank statement
savings	interest rate
withdrawal	exchange rate
deposit	to open a bank account
personal identification number (PIN)	to deposit/withdraw/exchange money

library

library building

City

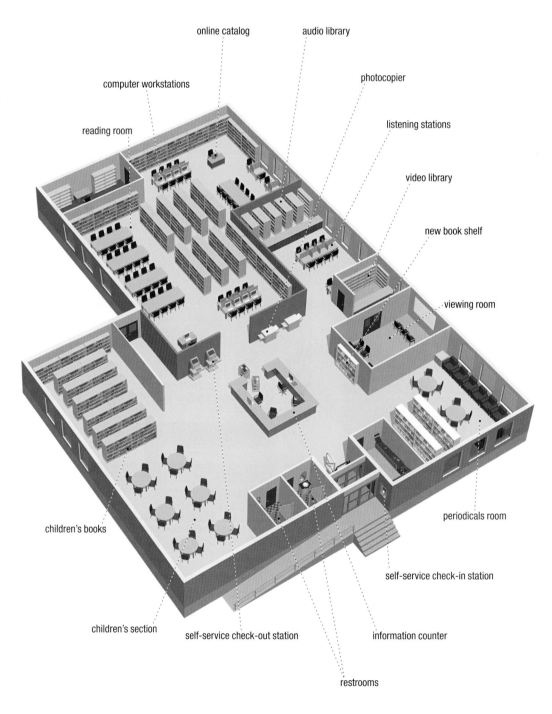

online catalog

audio library

computer workstations

photocopier

reading room

listening stations

video library

new book shelf

viewing room

children's books

periodicals room

self-service check-in station

children's section

self-service check-out station

information counter

restrooms

printed book

digital book

audio book

movie

music

comic book

illustrated book

magazine

City

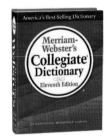

newspaper

dictionary

practical guide

novel

author

title

publisher

librarian
library card
due date
late fee
encyclopedia
fantasy novel
detective novel
adventure novel
romance
search
subject
keyword
to borrow/return
to renew a loan
I'm looking for…

City

clothing store

fitting room • seller

mirror • price tag

sale • customer/client • checkout counter • size

fabric	machine wash
cotton	wash in cold/lukewarm/warm water
silk	dry clean
wool	tumble dry
nylon	hang to dry
polyester	dry flat
low price	do not iron
high price	Let's go shopping.
quality	Do you have it in other colors?
second-hand clothes store	Do you have it in a smaller/larger size?
gift card	I would like to try it on.
final sale	Where can I find…
hand washable	Can I get an exchange or a refund?

City

departments

women's clothing

men's clothing

children's clothing

babies' wear

winter wear

summer wear

sportswear

maternity wear

nightclothes

underwear

swimsuits

casual wear

evening wear

women's suits

men's suits

headgear

scarves

gloves

belts

watches and jewelry

women's shoes

men's shoes

sports shoes

children's shoes

City

market

fruit and vegetable seller

open-air market

local product

organic product

farmers market

tasting

cheese shop

fish shop

butcher's shop

bakery

flower market

street food   food truck

ice cream parlor

chocolate shop

antique

second-hand merchandise

antique shop   **flea market**

grocery list
special offer
seasonal product
loose/bulk product
price per pound/kilo
nutritional value
line
reusable bag
sales tax
to shop
May I help you?
Do you have…
Can I taste…?
Anything else?

supermarket

general view

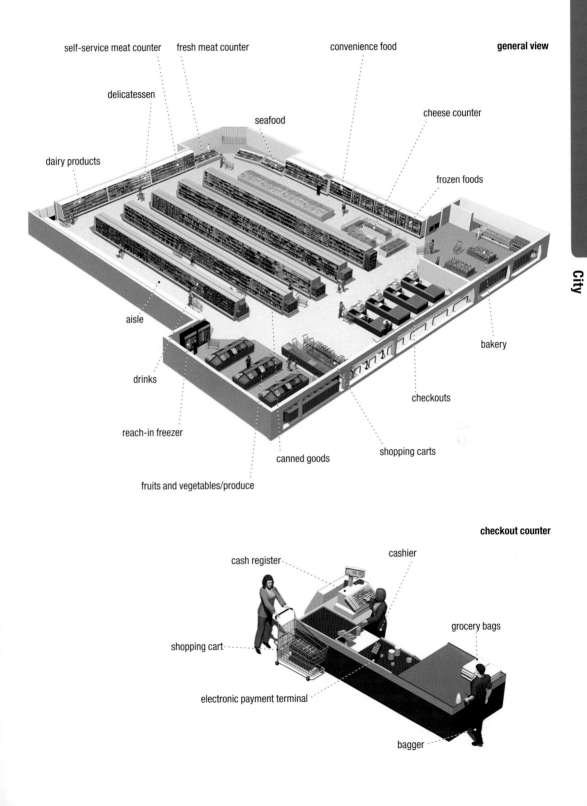

self-service meat counter

fresh meat counter

convenience food

delicatessen

cheese counter

seafood

dairy products

frozen foods

aisle

bakery

drinks

checkouts

reach-in freezer

canned goods

shopping carts

fruits and vegetables/produce

checkout counter

cash register

cashier

shopping cart

grocery bags

electronic payment terminal

bagger

City

restaurant and bar

general view

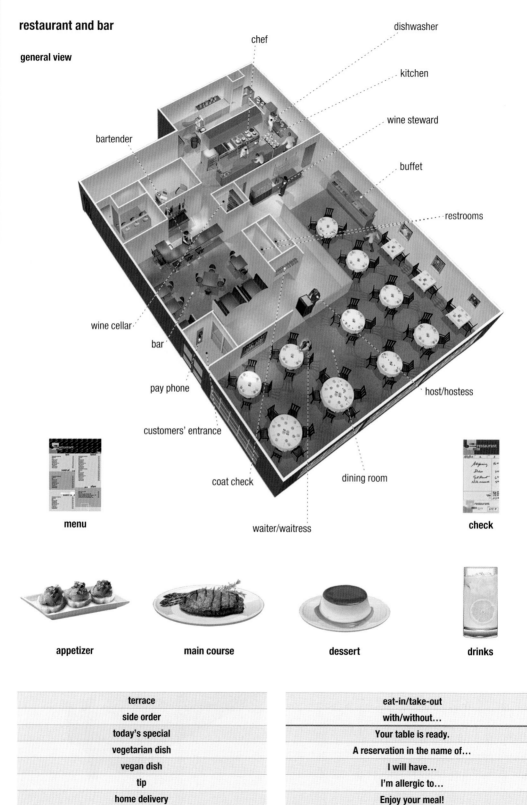

chef

dishwasher

kitchen

wine steward

buffet

restrooms

bartender

wine cellar

bar

pay phone

customers' entrance

coat check

dining room

host/hostess

waiter/waitress

menu

check

appetizer

main course

dessert

drinks

terrace	eat-in/take-out
side order	with/without...
today's special	Your table is ready.
vegetarian dish	A reservation in the name of...
vegan dish	I will have...
tip	I'm allergic to...
home delivery	Enjoy your meal!

hairdressing and beauty salon

hairdressing salon

hair dye

shampoo

hair dryer — hair styling product

hair stylist — haircutting scissors — mirror

drying

curls

depilatory wax

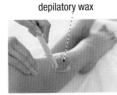

hair removal

foot care

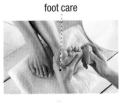

pedicure

barber

trimmer

barbershop

aesthetician

facial

beauty salon

nail care

manicure

haircut	highlights
shaving	layered cut
wig	curling iron
short hair	straightening iron
long hair	sensitive/dry/oily skin
dry/oily hair	nail polish
bangs	Do not cut too short.

City

movies

movie theater

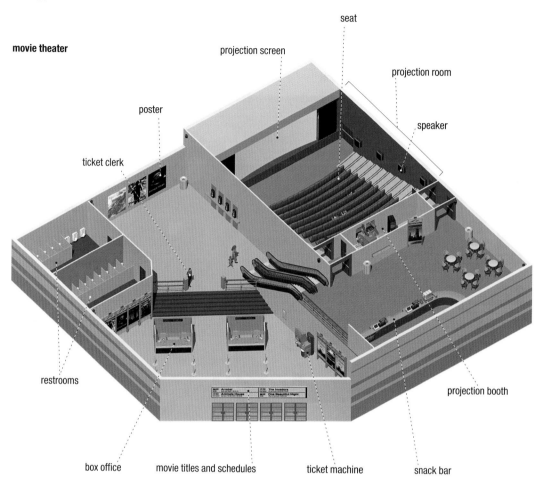

seat

projection screen

projection room

poster

speaker

ticket clerk

restrooms

box office

movie titles and schedules

ticket machine

snack bar

projection booth

actor

actress

movie

drama

comedy

trailer
original/dubbed/sub-titled version
documentary
animated movie
action movie
3D movie

science fiction

horror movie

parks and playgrounds

festival
carnival
amusement arcade
bowling alley
crowd
picnic

public garden

scenic overlook

botanical garden

zoo

aquarium

water park

amusement park

circus

Ferris wheel

acrobat

roller coaster · ride

clown · juggler

playground

modular play structure

swing · athletic field · tunnel · slide

In most countries, education is compulsory up to a certain age. Primary education, which starts around the ages of 5 to 7, is usually free. As well as learning to read, write and count, children develop all kinds of intellectual, physical, social and artistic skills in school. But a lack of resources means that many children in poor or war-torn countries will not get a formal education.

School

school

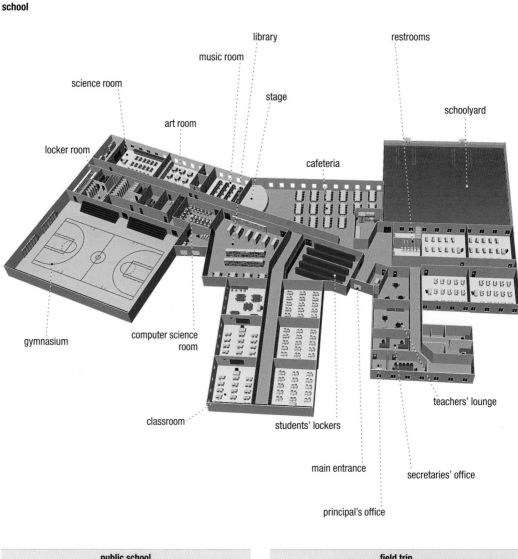

library

restrooms

music room

science room

stage

schoolyard

art room

cafeteria

locker room

gymnasium

computer science
room

classroom

students' lockers

teachers' lounge

main entrance

secretaries' office

principal's office

public school	field trip
private school	immersion class (language)
boarding school	special needs teacher
school uniform	educational psychologist
auditorium	to graduate
student council	to repeat a grade

kindergarten

elementary school (primary school)

high school (secondary school)

higher education

back-to-school time

school vacation

report card

diploma

School

cafeteria

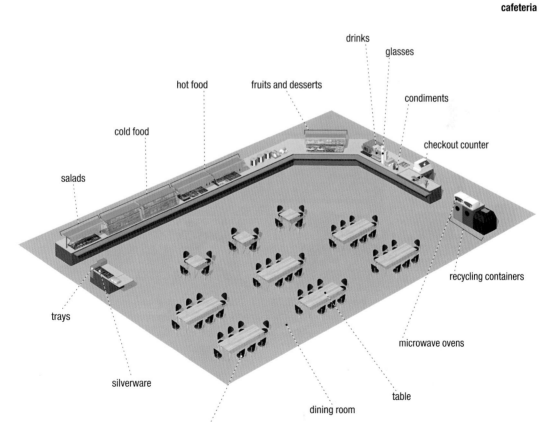

drinks

glasses

hot food

fruits and desserts

condiments

cold food

checkout counter

salads

trays

recycling containers

silverware

microwave ovens

chair

dining room

table

computer equipment

computer

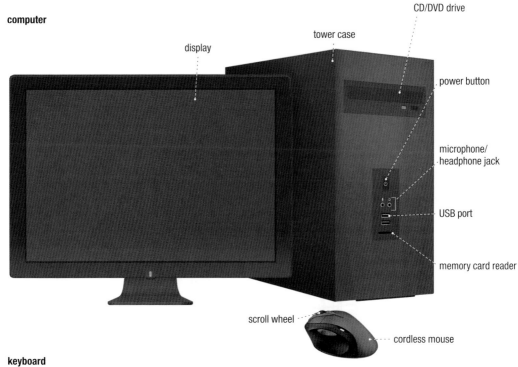

display

tower case

CD/DVD drive

power button

microphone/ headphone jack

USB port

memory card reader

scroll wheel

cordless mouse

keyboard

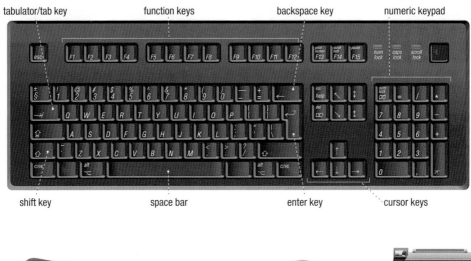

tabulator/tab key

function keys

backspace key

numeric keypad

shift key

space bar

enter key

cursor keys

external hard drive

USB flash drive

USB cable

multifunction printer

computer equipment

laptop computer

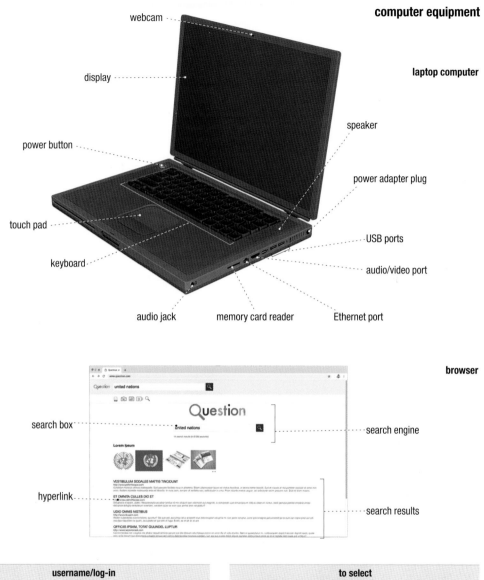

webcam

display

power button

touch pad

keyboard

speaker

power adapter plug

USB ports

audio/video port

audio jack

memory card reader

Ethernet port

browser

search box

hyperlink

search engine

search results

username/log-in	to select
password	to move
menu	to insert
task bar/tool bar	to copy/cut/paste
window	to cancel/undo
word processing software	to save
presentation software	to delete
e-mail	to search by keyword
to start	to bookmark
to shut down	to send an email
to type	to receive an email
to click	to send as an attachment
	to download a file

Biology is the science of living organisms. Since the first single-celled forms appeared on Earth about 3.5 billion years ago, life has evolved enormously with millions of diverse species now occupying the planet. We use a system called taxonomy to describe and classify living things based on shared characteristics.

School

biological classification: cat

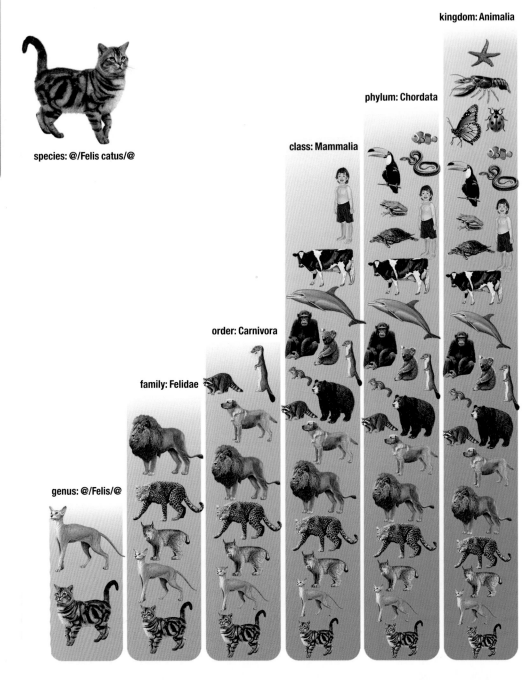

kingdom: Animalia

phylum: Chordata

class: Mammalia

order: Carnivora

family: Felidae

genus: @/Felis/@

species: @/Felis catus/@

laboratory

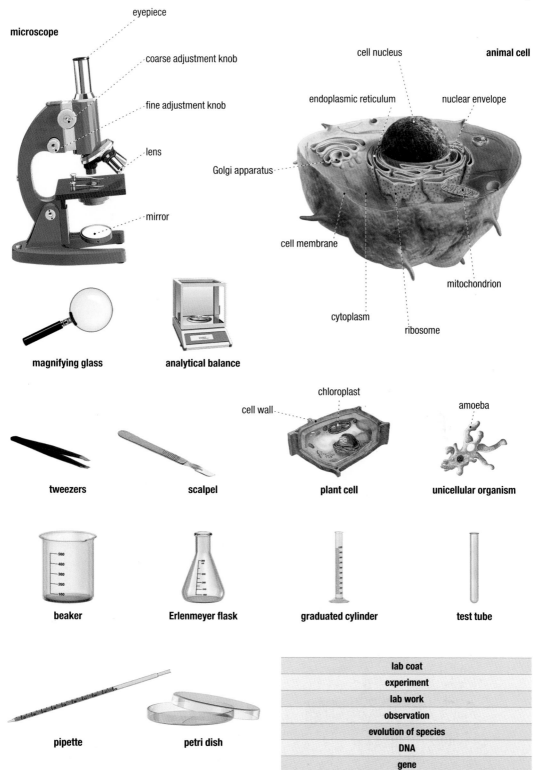

microscope

eyepiece

coarse adjustment knob

fine adjustment knob

lens

mirror

magnifying glass

analytical balance

animal cell

cell nucleus

endoplasmic reticulum

nuclear envelope

Golgi apparatus

cell membrane

mitochondrion

cytoplasm

ribosome

tweezers

scalpel

cell wall

chloroplast

plant cell

amoeba

unicellular organism

beaker

Erlenmeyer flask

graduated cylinder

test tube

pipette

petri dish

| lab coat |
| experiment |
| lab work |
| observation |
| evolution of species |
| DNA |
| gene |

School

School

Plants and plantlike organisms vary in size, structure, and means of reproduction. Some, like trees, are large and produce seeds from flowers or cones. Others, like mosses, are very small with tiny leaves and produce spores instead of seeds. Although mushrooms resemble plants, they are fungi incapable of photosynthesis and are classified in a separate kingdom.

plant and plantlike diversity

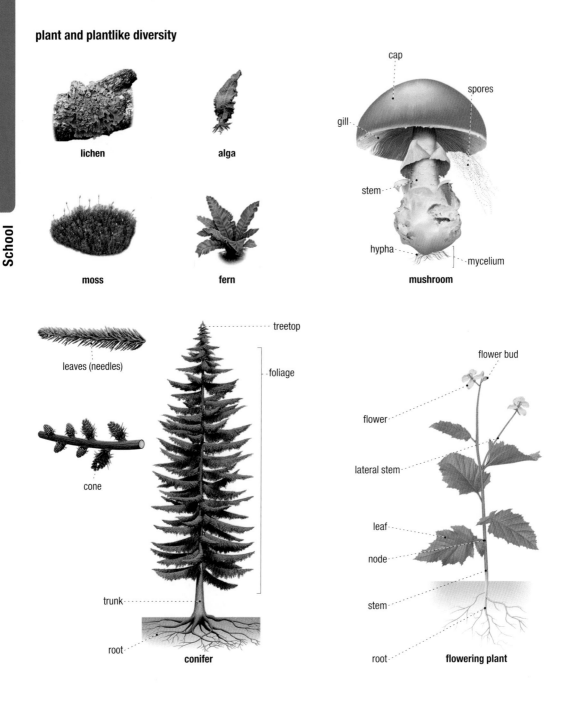

lichen

alga

cap

spores

gill

stem

hypha

mycelium

moss

fern

mushroom

treetop

leaves (needles)

foliage

cone

flower bud

flower

lateral stem

leaf

node

trunk

stem

root

root

conifer

flowering plant

photosynthesis

nutrition and reproduction

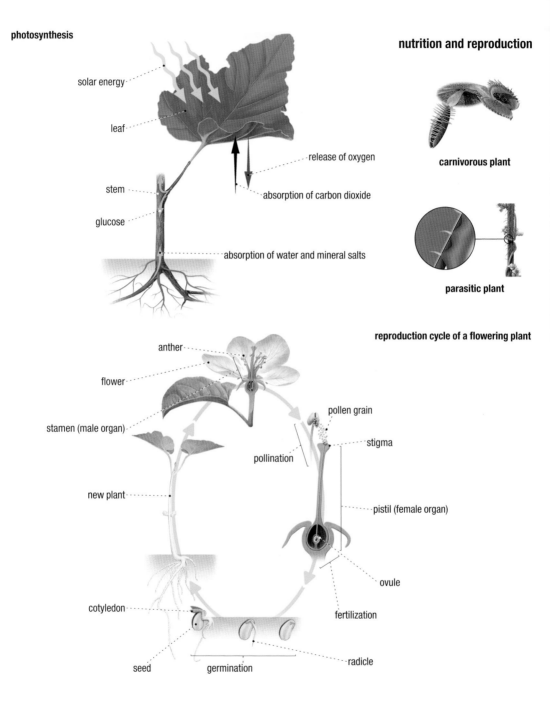

solar energy

leaf

stem

glucose

release of oxygen

absorption of carbon dioxide

absorption of water and mineral salts

carnivorous plant

parasitic plant

reproduction cycle of a flowering plant

anther

flower

stamen (male organ)

new plant

cotyledon

seed

germination

pollen grain

stigma

pollination

pistil (female organ)

ovule

fertilization

radicle

flowering	deciduous foliage
sap	evergreen foliage
annual plant	to sprout
perennial plant	to grow
climbing plant	to flower
stinging plant	to scatter
weed	to wilt

structure of a flower

petal

lily

corolla

peduncle

stigma

style

ovary

ovule

pistil (female organ)

anther

pollen

stamen (male organ)

examples of flowers

tulip

daisy

sunflower

rose

dandelion

poppy

thistle

crocus

buttercup

violet

primrose

lily of the valley

daffodil

carnation

geranium

orchid

examples of broadleaved trees

palm tree

poplar

birch

rubber tree

oak

weeping willow

maple

walnut

linden

elm

beech

ash

baobab

acacia

olive tree

examples of conifers

umbrella pine

cedar of Lebanon

cypress

spruce

larch/tamarack

redwood

eastern white pine

fir

use of plants

fruit production

fruit

orchard

sugar cane

sugar industry

white sugar

brown sugar

vegetable production

vegetable garden

vegetable

grain industry

flour

vegetable oil

cereal

chocolate industry

cacao bean

cacao tree

chocolate

cotton plant

textile industry

clothing

wood and paper industry

paper

tree

lumber

rubber tree

rubber industry

latex harvest

ball

School

The first animals had soft bodies (invertebrates) and lived in water. The appearance of amphibians and later reptiles was due to the development of air-breathing lungs enabling life on land. Over millions of years, various animals (mollusks, crustaceans, insects) evolved with specialized structures like shells, wings, and jointed legs. Birds and mammals were the last type of life forms to appear on Earth.

origin and evolution of species

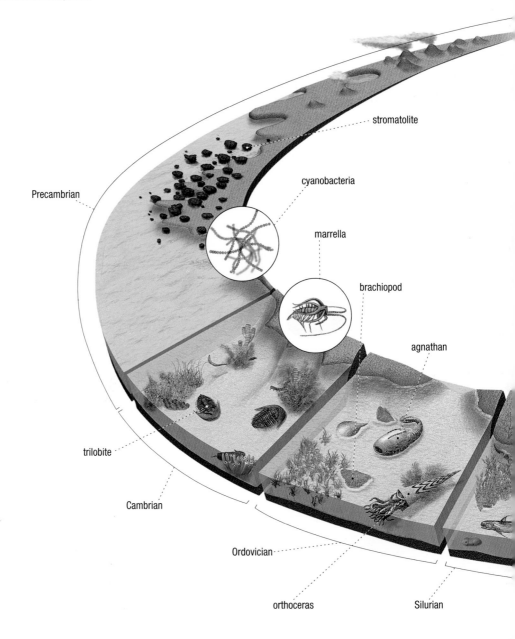

stromatolite

cyanobacteria

Precambrian

marrella

brachiopod

agnathan

trilobite

Cambrian

Ordovician

orthoceras

Silurian

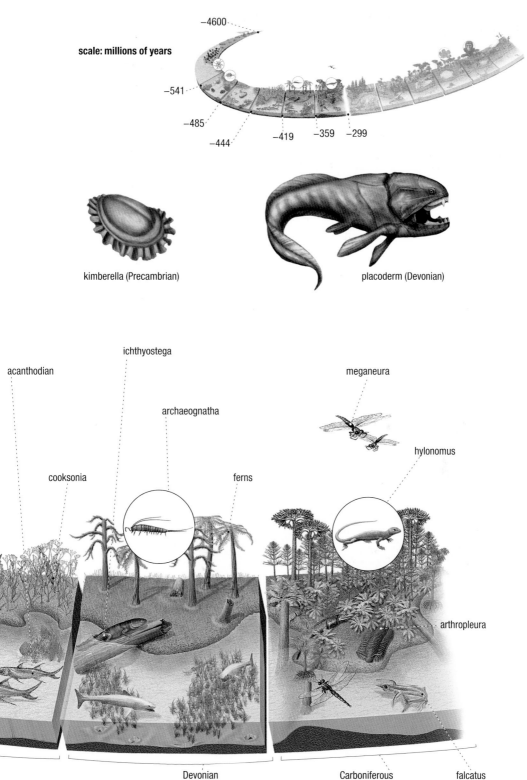

scale: millions of years

−4600
−541
−485
−444
−419
−359
−299

kimberella (Precambrian)

placoderm (Devonian)

acanthodian

ichthyostega

archaeognatha

meganeura

hylonomus

cooksonia

ferns

arthropleura

Devonian

Carboniferous

falcatus

origin and evolution of species

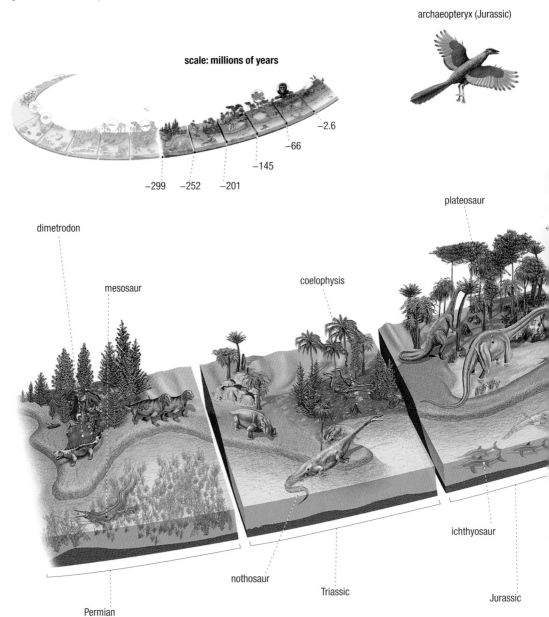

archaeopteryx (Jurassic)

scale: millions of years

−2.6

−66

−145

−299   −252   −201

dimetrodon

mesosaur

coelophysis

plateosaur

ichthyosaur

nothosaur

Triassic

Jurassic

Permian

megazostrodon (Triassic)

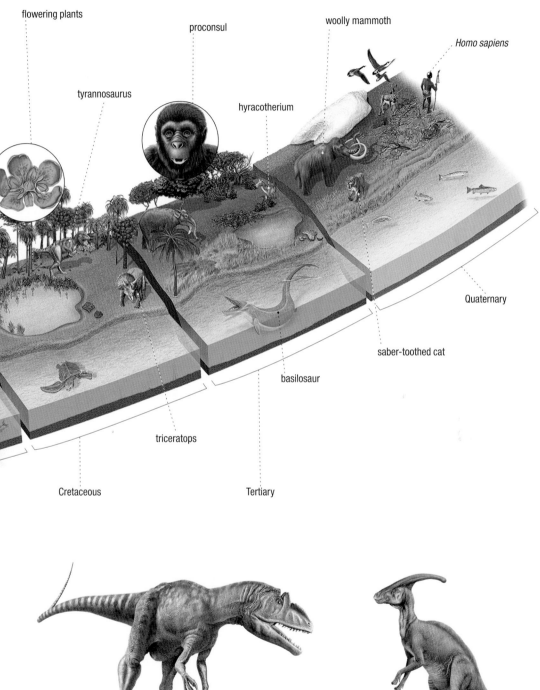

flowering plants

tyrannosaurus

proconsul

hyracotherium

woolly mammoth

Homo sapiens

Quaternary

saber-toothed cat

basilosaur

triceratops

Cretaceous

Tertiary

allosaurus (Jurassic)

parasaurolophus (Cretaceous)

School

primitive animals

sponge

jellyfish

starfish

anemone

sea urchin

sea cucumber

coral

earthworm

mollusks

oyster

bivalve shell

mussel

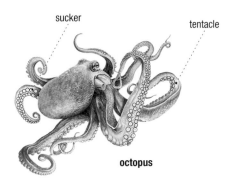

sucker   tentacle

octopus

slug

univalve shell

whelk

squid   cuttlefish

shell

eye

snail

periwinkle

limpet

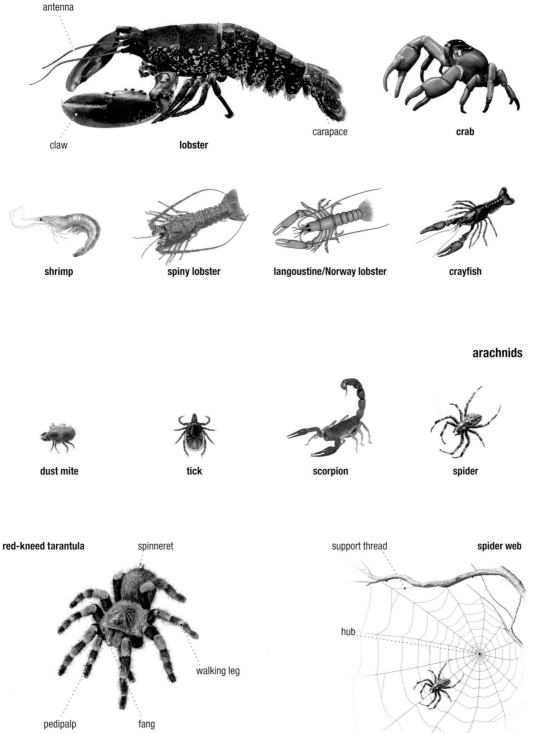

crustaceans

antenna

claw   **lobster**   carapace   **crab**

shrimp   **spiny lobster**   **langoustine/Norway lobster**   **crayfish**

School

arachnids

dust mite   **tick**   **scorpion**   **spider**

red-kneed tarantula   spinneret   support thread   **spider web**

walking leg

hub

pedipalp   fang

insects

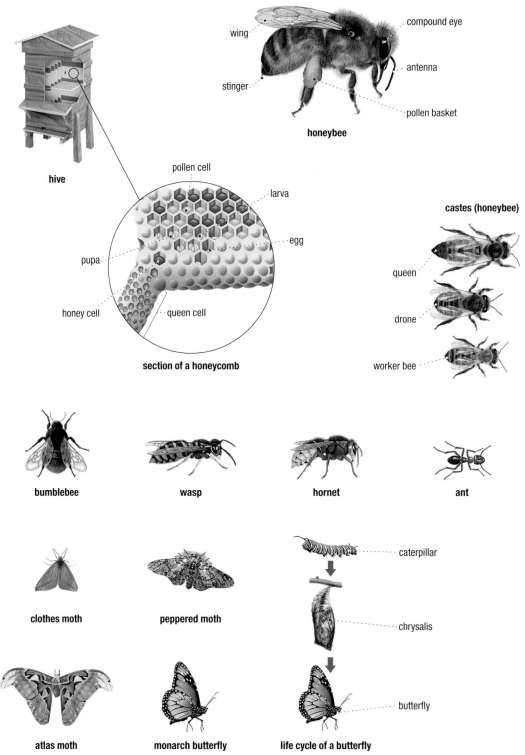

hive

wing

compound eye

stinger

antenna

pollen basket

honeybee

pollen cell

larva

egg

pupa

honey cell

queen cell

section of a honeycomb

castes (honeybee)

queen

drone

worker bee

bumblebee

wasp

hornet

ant

clothes moth

peppered moth

caterpillar

chrysalis

butterfly

atlas moth

monarch butterfly

life cycle of a butterfly

insects

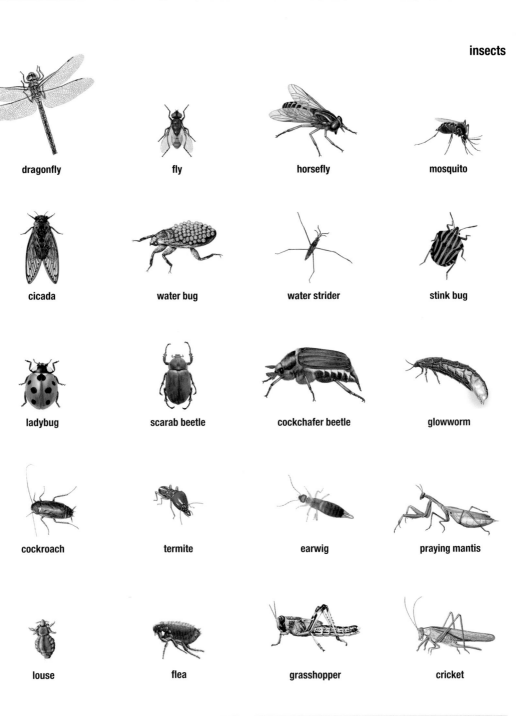

dragonfly

fly

horsefly

mosquito

cicada

water bug

water strider

stink bug

ladybug

scarab beetle

cockchafer beetle

glowworm

cockroach

termite

earwig

praying mantis

louse

flea

grasshopper

cricket

butterfly	anthill
moth	swarn
gnat	pest
sting	infestation
bite	parasite
venom	bed bug
social insect	to fly

School

fishes

shark

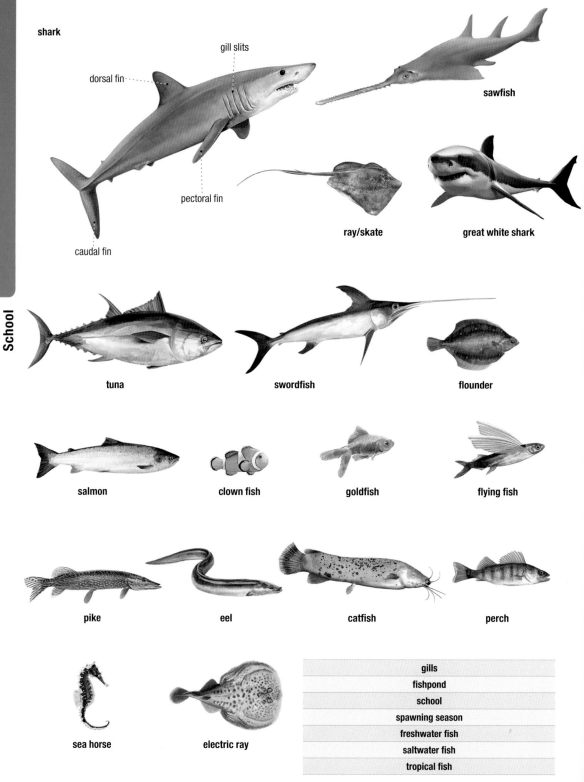

gill slits

dorsal fin

pectoral fin

caudal fin

sawfish

ray/skate

great white shark

tuna

swordfish

flounder

salmon

clown fish

goldfish

flying fish

pike

eel

catfish

perch

sea horse

electric ray

gills
fishpond
school
spawning season
freshwater fish
saltwater fish
tropical fish

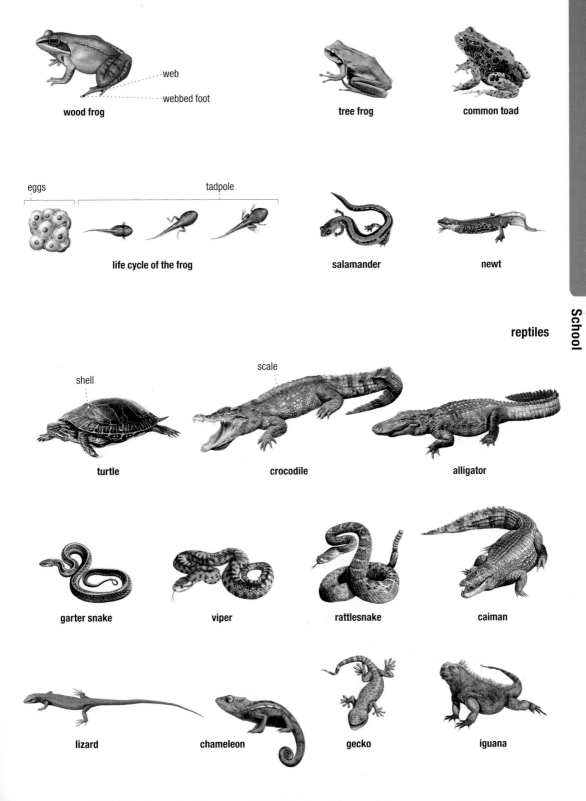

amphibians

web
webbed foot
wood frog

tree frog

common toad

eggs
tadpole
life cycle of the frog

salamander

newt

reptiles

School

shell
turtle

scale
crocodile

alligator

garter snake

viper

rattlesnake

caiman

lizard

chameleon

gecko

iguana

School

birds

nightingale

wing

bill

feather

great horned owl

eagle

woodpecker

talon

falcon

sparrow

cardinal

swallow

goldfinch

finch

raven

jay

European robin

pigeon

partridge

pheasant

ostrich

turkey

hen

chick

rooster

birds

peacock

macaw

toucan

hummingbird

penguin

flamingo

stork

heron

auk

gull

tern

albatross

pelican

swan

goose

duck

kingfisher

oystercatcher

| ornithology |
| migratory bird |
| bird of prey |
| shorebird |
| plumage/feathers |
| nest/nesting |
| egg-laying |

School

School

marsupial mammals

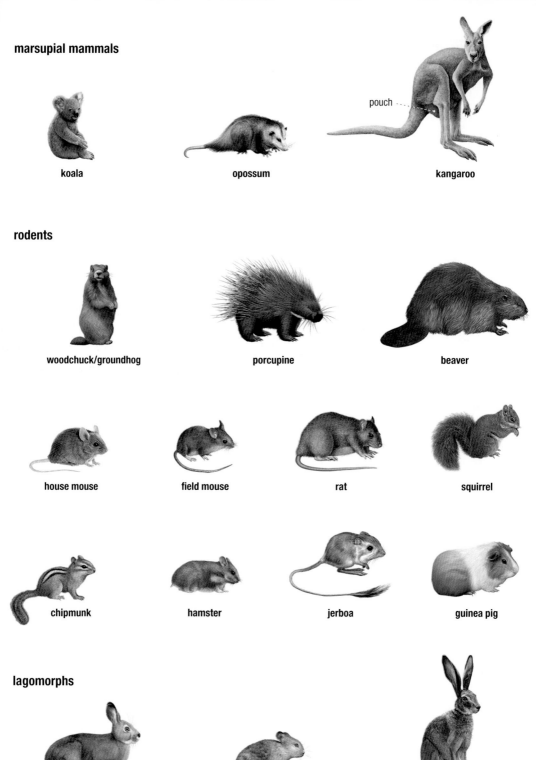

koala

opossum

pouch

kangaroo

rodents

woodchuck/groundhog

porcupine

beaver

house mouse

field mouse

rat

squirrel

chipmunk

hamster

jerboa

guinea pig

lagomorphs

rabbit

pika

hare

ungulate mammals

tusk

elephant

giraffe

rhinoceros

hippopotamus

sheep

goat

cow

ox

pig

wild boar

bison

Cape buffalo

bighorn sheep

antlers

caribou

deer

hoof

moose

School

dromedary camel

Bactrian camel

antelope

llama

donkey

mule

horse

zebra

School

insectivorous mammals

mole

hedgehog

shrew

bat

carnivorous mammals

badger

raccoon

river otter

wolf

fox

skunk

weasel

hyena

black bear (omnivore)

polar bear

tiger

leopard

cheetah

lion

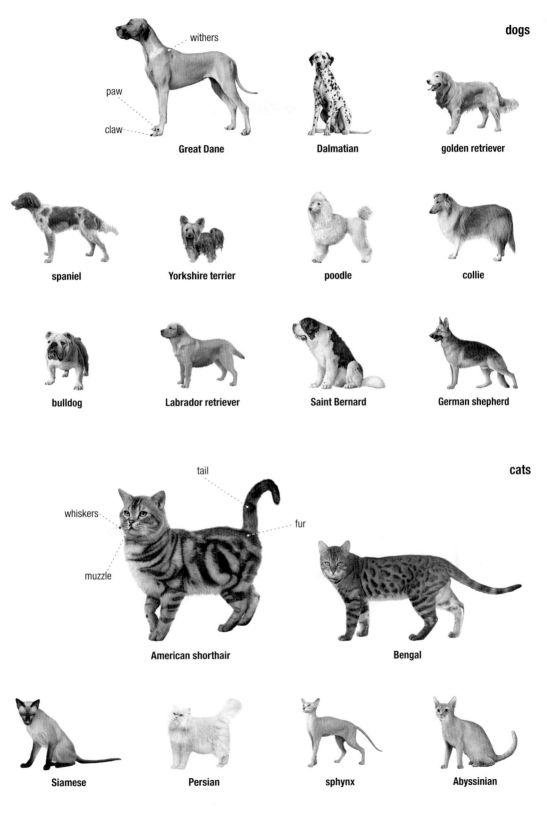

dogs

withers

paw

claw

Great Dane

Dalmatian

golden retriever

spaniel

Yorkshire terrier

poodle

collie

bulldog

Labrador retriever

Saint Bernard

German shepherd

School

cats

tail

whiskers

fur

muzzle

American shorthair

Bengal

Siamese

Persian

sphynx

Abyssinian

No life-forms are found outside the very thin layer of earth, air and water called the biosphere. That habitable part of our planet is a complex world where the various species depend on one another for food. Some natural processes, like the hydrologic cycle, help make the environment suitable for life, whereas pollution degrades the biosphere.

structure of the biosphere

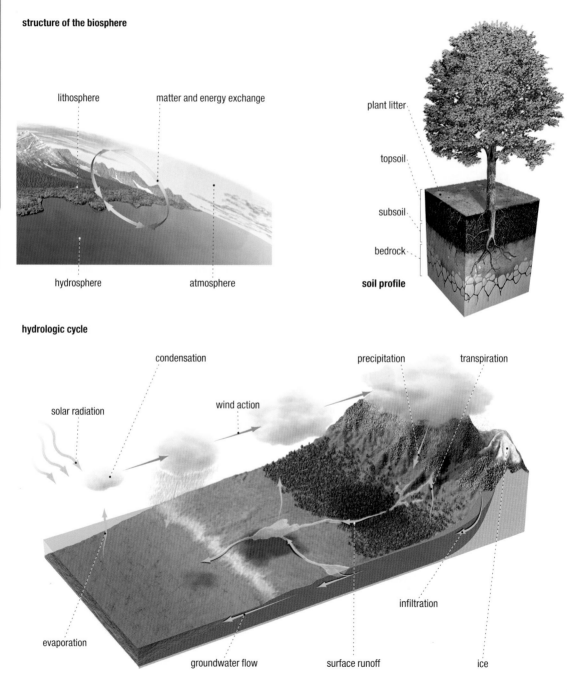

lithosphere

matter and energy exchange

plant litter

topsoil

subsoil

bedrock

hydrosphere

atmosphere

soil profile

hydrologic cycle

condensation

precipitation

transpiration

solar radiation

wind action

infiltration

evaporation

groundwater flow

surface runoff

ice

ecological pyramid

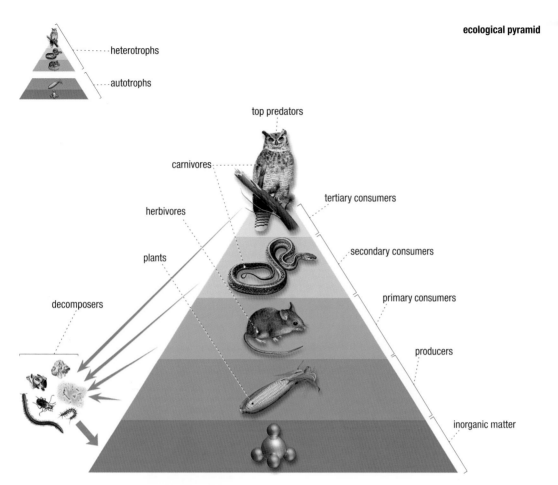

heterotrophs

autotrophs

top predators

carnivores

tertiary consumers

herbivores

secondary consumers

plants

primary consumers

decomposers

producers

inorganic matter

example of food chain

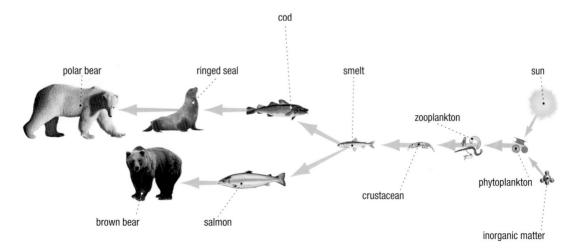

cod

polar bear

ringed seal

smelt

sun

zooplankton

phytoplankton

crustacean

brown bear

salmon

inorganic matter

School

vegetation regions

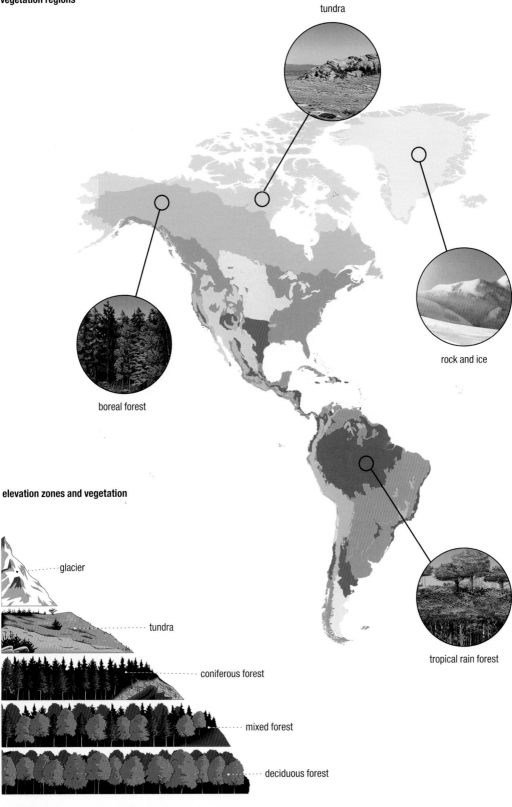

tundra

rock and ice

boreal forest

tropical rain forest

elevation zones and vegetation

glacier

tundra

coniferous forest

mixed forest

deciduous forest

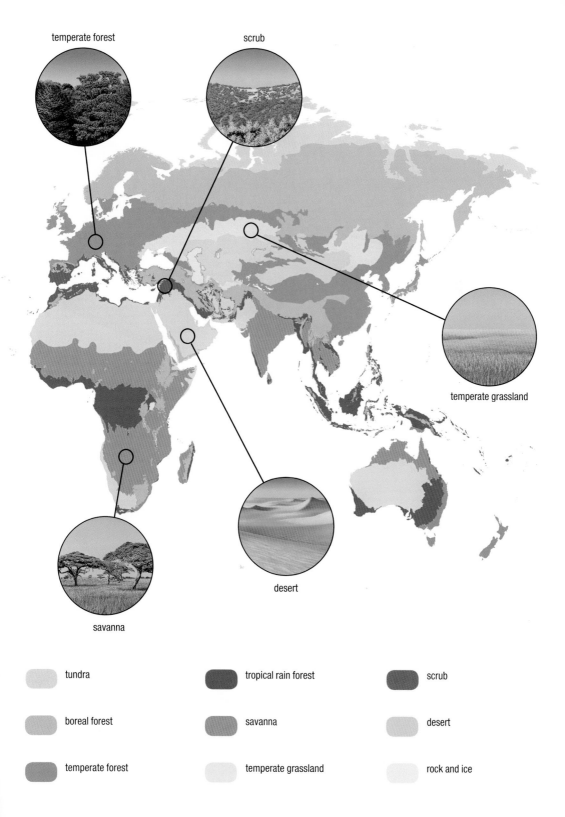

temperate forest

scrub

temperate grassland

School

savanna

desert

tundra

tropical rain forest

scrub

boreal forest

savanna

desert

temperate forest

temperate grassland

rock and ice

School

natural greenhouse effect

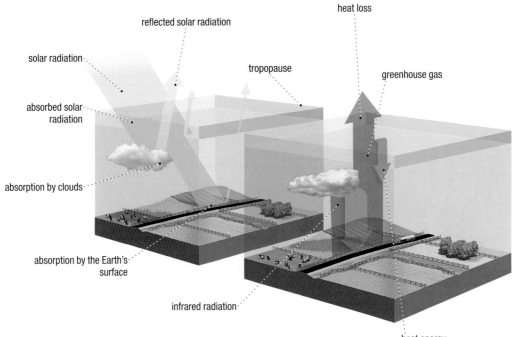

reflected solar radiation

heat loss

solar radiation

tropopause

greenhouse gas

absorbed solar radiation

absorption by clouds

absorption by the Earth's surface

infrared radiation

heat energy

enhanced greenhouse effect

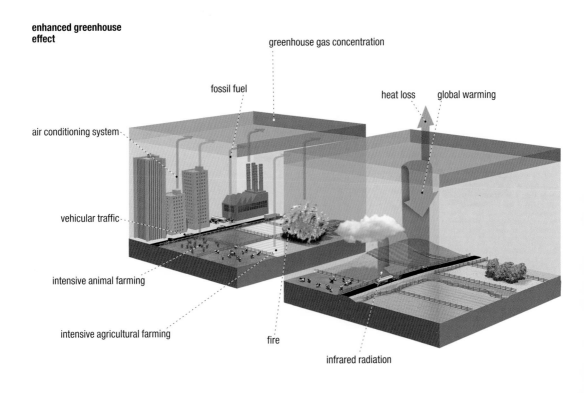

greenhouse gas concentration

fossil fuel

heat loss

global warming

air conditioning system

vehicular traffic

intensive animal farming

intensive agricultural farming

fire

infrared radiation

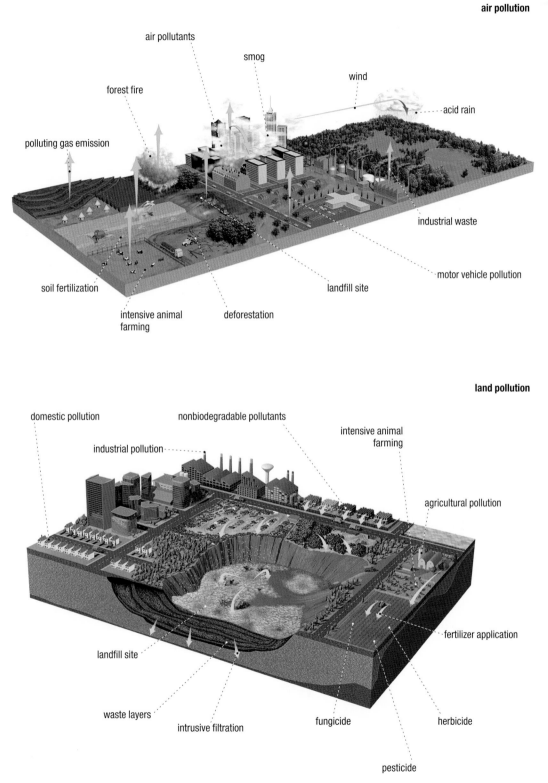

air pollutants

smog

wind

forest fire

acid rain

polluting gas emission

industrial waste

soil fertilization

motor vehicle pollution

landfill site

intensive animal
farming

deforestation

School

domestic pollution

nonbiodegradable pollutants

intensive animal
farming

industrial pollution

agricultural pollution

fertilizer application

landfill site

waste layers

intrusive filtration

fungicide

herbicide

pesticide

water pollution

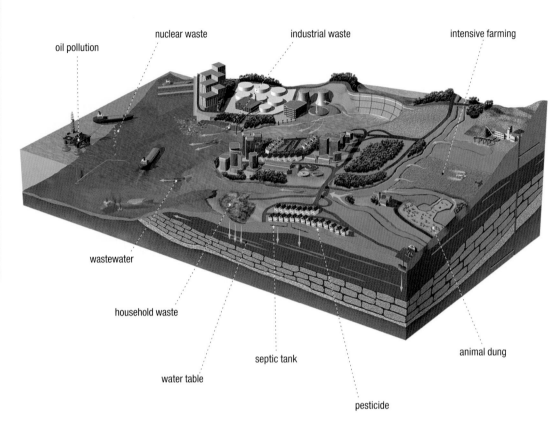

oil pollution

nuclear waste

industrial waste

intensive farming

wastewater

household waste

water table

septic tank

pesticide

animal dung

environmental protection measures

clean energy production

public transportation

green transportation

recycling

local purchase

organic farming

reforestation

protected areas

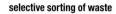

selective sorting of waste

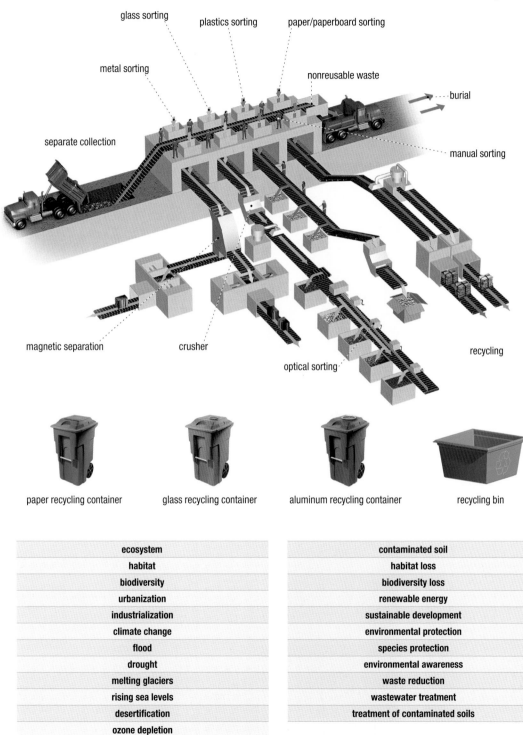

glass sorting

plastics sorting

paper/paperboard sorting

metal sorting

nonreusable waste

burial

separate collection

manual sorting

magnetic separation

crusher

recycling

optical sorting

School

paper recycling container

glass recycling container

aluminum recycling container

recycling bin

ecosystem	contaminated soil
habitat	habitat loss
biodiversity	biodiversity loss
urbanization	renewable energy
industrialization	sustainable development
climate change	environmental protection
flood	species protection
drought	environmental awareness
melting glaciers	waste reduction
rising sea levels	wastewater treatment
desertification	treatment of contaminated soils
ozone depletion	

Meteorology is the study of the phenomena that occur in the atmosphere and especially weather and weather forecasting. The many different weather stations use instruments that measure things like wind direction, air humidity and atmospheric pressure. Meteorologists can use their findings to predict the weather in the days ahead.

profile of the Earth's atmosphere

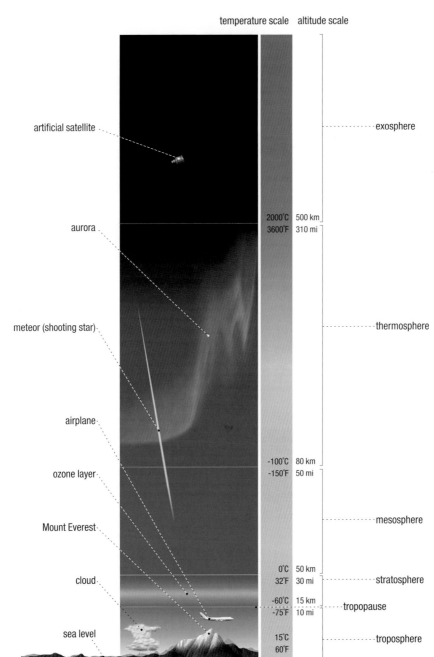

temperature scale   altitude scale

artificial satellite .... exosphere

2000°C 500 km
3600°F 310 mi

aurora

thermosphere

meteor (shooting star)

airplane

-100°C 80 km
-150°F 50 mi

ozone layer

mesosphere

Mount Everest

0°C   50 km
32°F 30 mi .... stratosphere

cloud

-60°C 15 km
-75°F 10 mi .... tropopause

sea level

15°C
60°F .... troposphere

clouds

high clouds

middle clouds

low clouds

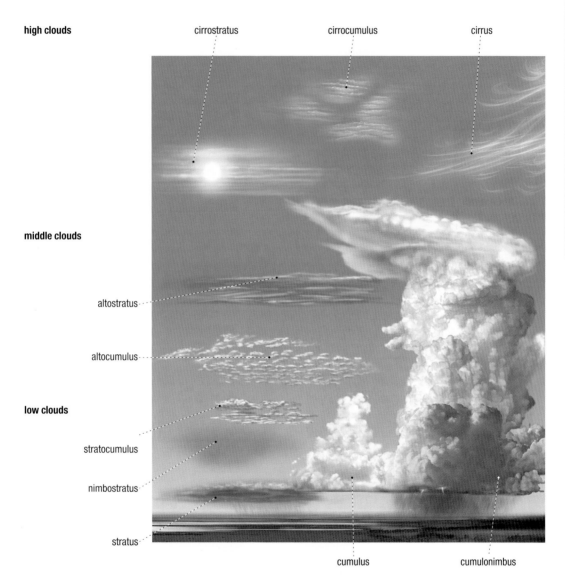

cirrostratus — cirrocumulus — cirrus

altostratus

altocumulus

stratocumulus

nimbostratus

stratus

cumulus — cumulonimbus

weather	cloudy weather
shower	windy weather
snowstorm	humid weather
gust of wind	dry weather
thunder	heat wave
nice/bad weather	What's the weather like?
rainy weather	Is it going to rain?

climates of the world

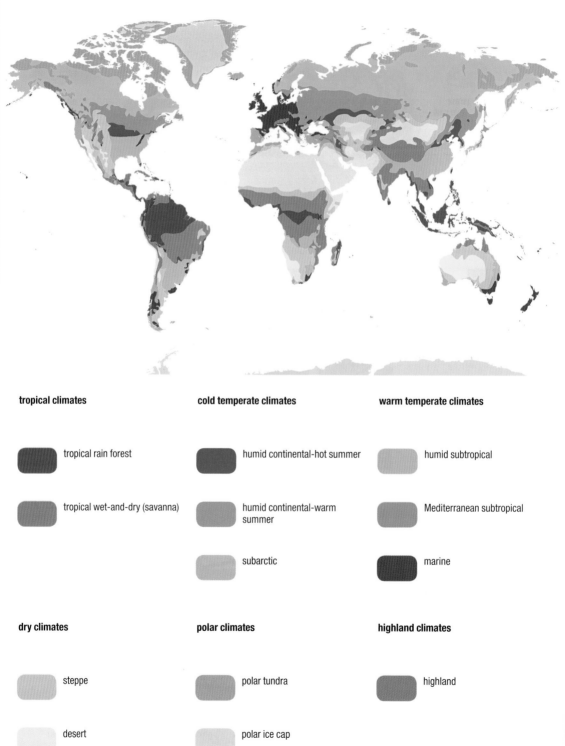

tropical climates

tropical rain forest

tropical wet-and-dry (savanna)

cold temperate climates

humid continental-hot summer

humid continental-warm summer

subarctic

warm temperate climates

humid subtropical

Mediterranean subtropical

marine

dry climates

steppe

desert

polar climates

polar tundra

polar ice cap

highland climates

highland

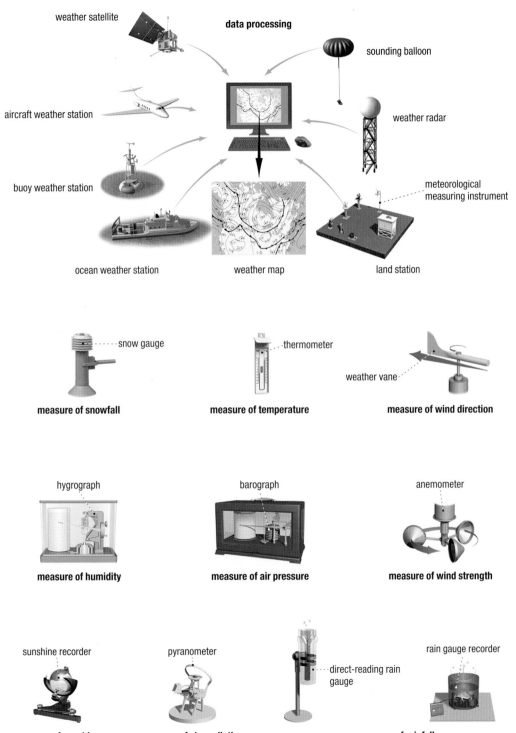

weather forecast

weather satellite

data processing

sounding balloon

aircraft weather station

weather radar

buoy weather station

meteorological measuring instrument

ocean weather station

weather map

land station

snow gauge

measure of snowfall

thermometer

measure of temperature

weather vane

measure of wind direction

hygrograph

measure of humidity

barograph

measure of air pressure

anemometer

measure of wind strength

sunshine recorder

measure of sunshine

pyranometer

measure of sky radiation

direct-reading rain gauge

rain gauge recorder

measure of rainfall

Our Earth is made up of three main layers: the crust, the mantle and the core. The crust is mainly rock and is divided into immense pieces called tectonic plates. Earthquakes and volcanic eruptions often happen at the meeting point of two plates. These phenomena contribute to the evolution of the landscapes.

structure of the Earth

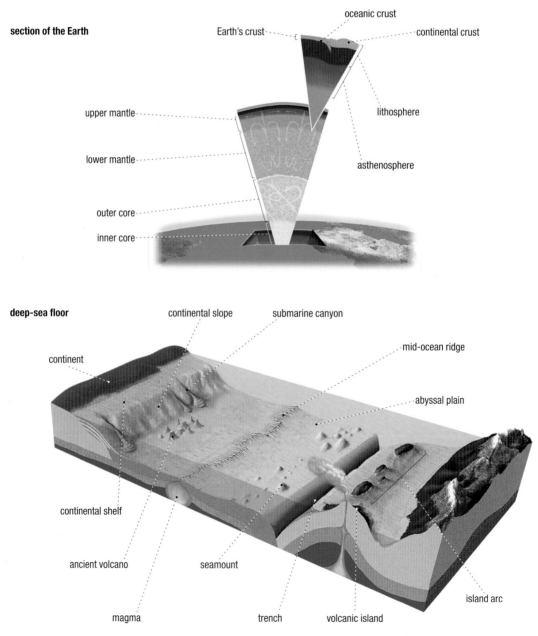

section of the Earth

oceanic crust

Earth's crust

continental crust

upper mantle

lithosphere

lower mantle

asthenosphere

outer core

inner core

deep-sea floor

continental slope   submarine canyon

mid-ocean ridge

continent

abyssal plain

continental shelf

ancient volcano   seamount

island arc

magma   trench   volcanic island

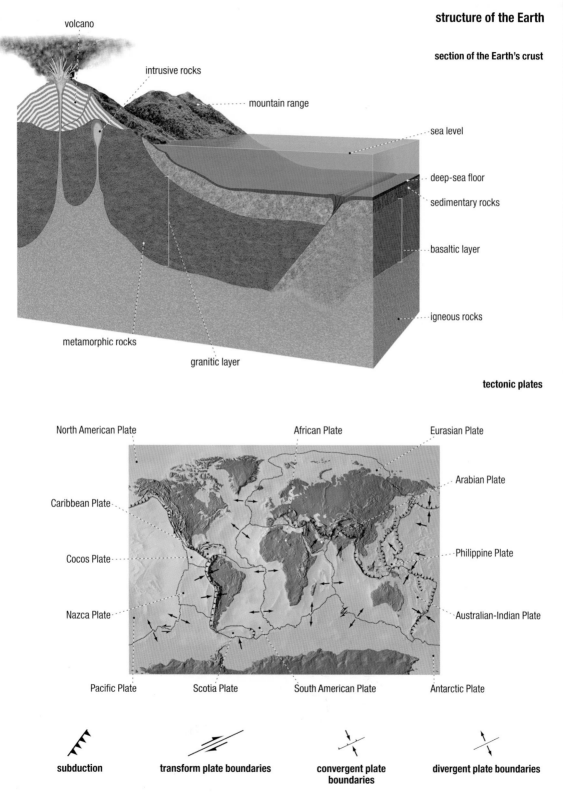

structure of the Earth

section of the Earth's crust

volcano

intrusive rocks

mountain range

sea level

deep-sea floor

sedimentary rocks

basaltic layer

igneous rocks

metamorphic rocks

granitic layer

School

tectonic plates

North American Plate

African Plate

Eurasian Plate

Arabian Plate

Caribbean Plate

Cocos Plate

Philippine Plate

Nazca Plate

Australian-Indian Plate

Pacific Plate

Scotia Plate

South American Plate

Antarctic Plate

subduction

transform plate boundaries

convergent plate boundaries

divergent plate boundaries

Earth features

School

mountain

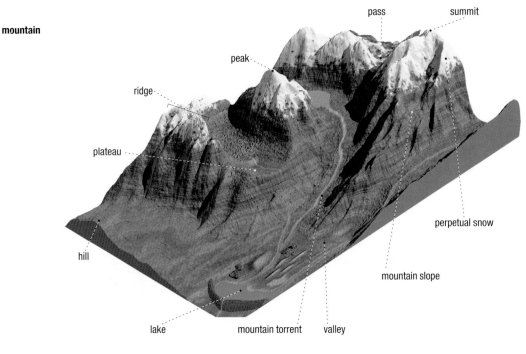

pass

summit

peak

ridge

plateau

hill

lake

mountain torrent

valley

mountain slope

perpetual snow

mountain formation

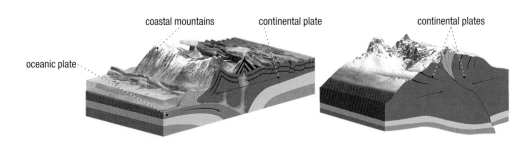

coastal mountains

continental plate

continental plates

oceanic plate

cave

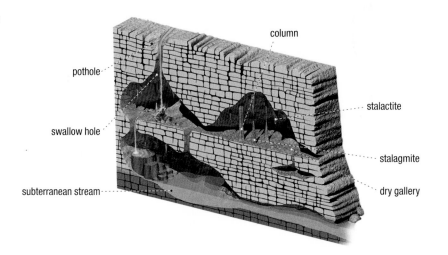

column

pothole

swallow hole

subterranean stream

stalactite

stalagmite

dry gallery

Earth features

watercourse

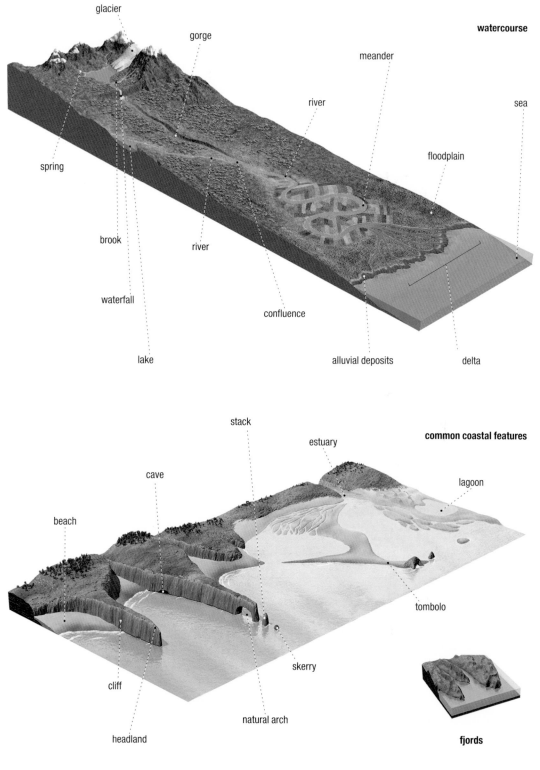

glacier

gorge

meander

river

sea

spring

floodplain

brook

river

waterfall

confluence

lake

alluvial deposits

delta

common coastal features

stack

estuary

cave

lagoon

beach

tombolo

skerry

cliff

natural arch

headland

fjords

Earth features

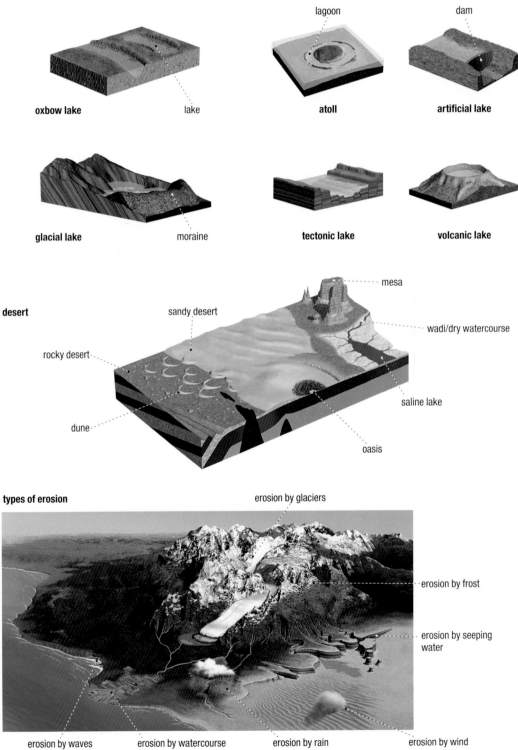

oxbow lake   lake

lagoon

dam

atoll

artificial lake

glacial lake   moraine

tectonic lake

volcanic lake

desert

mesa

sandy desert

rocky desert

wadi/dry watercourse

dune

saline lake

oasis

types of erosion

erosion by glaciers

erosion by frost

erosion by seeping water

erosion by waves   erosion by watercourse   erosion by rain   erosion by wind

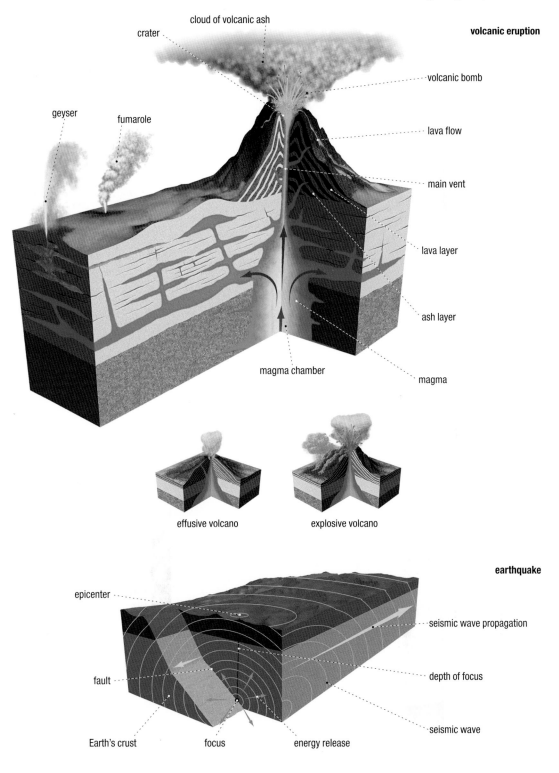

geological phenomena

volcanic eruption

cloud of volcanic ash

crater

volcanic bomb

lava flow

geyser

fumarole

main vent

lava layer

ash layer

magma chamber

magma

effusive volcano

explosive volcano

earthquake

epicenter

seismic wave propagation

fault

depth of focus

Earth's crust

focus

energy release

seismic wave

School

geological phenomena

tsunami

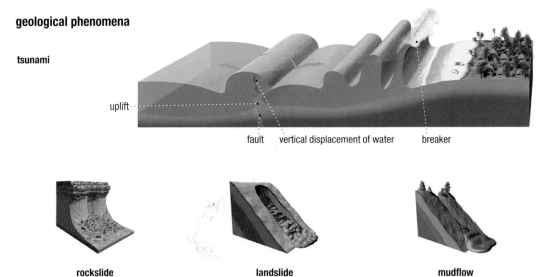

uplift

fault   vertical displacement of water   breaker

rockslide   landslide   mudflow

examples of rocks

igneous rocks — granite

basalt

pumice

sandstone

coal   **sedimentary rocks**

chalk   limestone

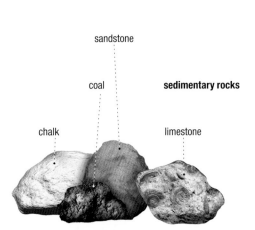

metamorphic rocks

marble

gneiss

slate

continental drift
seismograph
coast
tremor
shoreline
iceberg
hot spring
sediment
fossil
gem
hardness
luster
transparency
ore

examples of minerals

rock salt (halite)

calcite

graphite

pyrite

talc

feldspar

quartz

mica

examples of metals

School

iron

aluminum

copper

gold

silver

nickel

zinc

bronze = copper + tin

metal alloy

precious stones

sapphire

diamond

ruby

emerald

Our world is divided into huge areas of land surrounded by water, which are called continents. Eurasia is the continent formed by Europe and Asia combined. The continents cover about one-third of the surface of the globe. To represent the Earth's surface, cartographers draw maps that show, in detail, the different features of a given region. They use a projection system that will allow three-dimensional reality to be shown as a flat, two-dimensional map.

Earth coordinate system

grid system

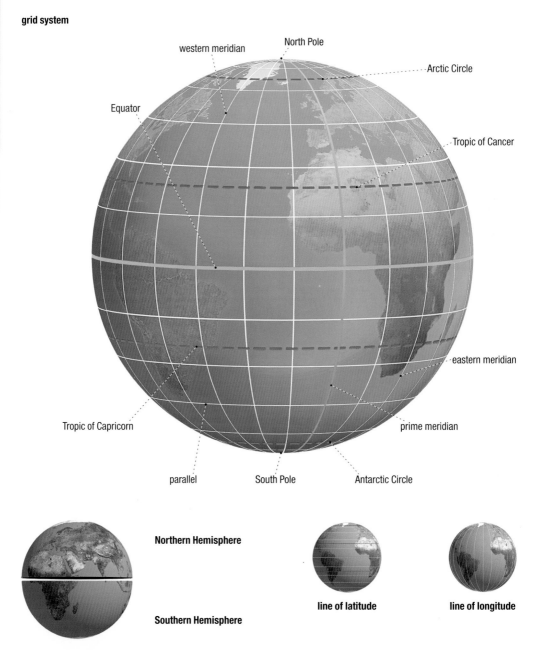

western meridian

North Pole

Arctic Circle

Equator

Tropic of Cancer

eastern meridian

prime meridian

Tropic of Capricorn

parallel

South Pole

Antarctic Circle

Northern Hemisphere

Southern Hemisphere

line of latitude

line of longitude

School

configuration of the continents

planisphere

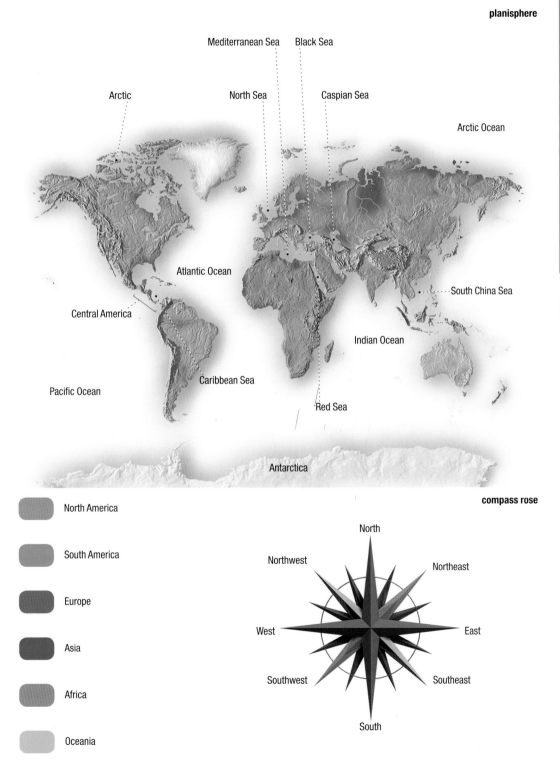

Mediterranean Sea   Black Sea

Arctic   North Sea   Caspian Sea

Arctic Ocean

Atlantic Ocean

Central America

South China Sea

Indian Ocean

Caribbean Sea

Pacific Ocean

Red Sea

Antarctica

compass rose

North America

South America

Europe

Asia

Africa

Oceania

North

Northwest   Northeast

West   East

Southwest   Southeast

South

School

cartography

physical map

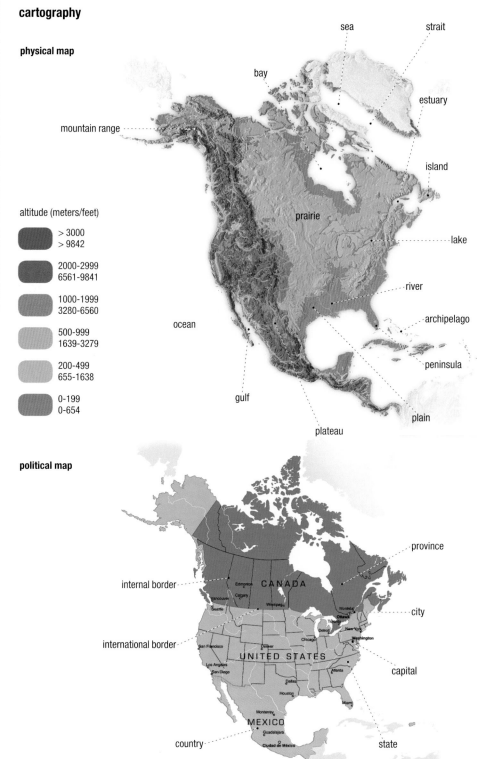

sea

strait

bay

estuary

mountain range

island

prairie

lake

altitude (meters/feet)

river

> 3000
> 9842

2000-2999
6561-9841

archipelago

1000-1999
3280-6560

ocean

500-999
1639-3279

peninsula

200-499
655-1638

gulf

0-199
0-654

plain

plateau

political map

province

internal border

Edmonton   CANADA

Vancouver
Calgary

city

Seattle   Winnipeg

Montréal

Ottawa
Toronto

international border

San Francisco   Denver

Detroit   New York

Chicago

Washington

UNITED STATES

Los Angeles

capital

San Diego

Atlanta

Dallas

Houston

Miami

Monterrey

MEXICO

country

Guadalajara

state

Ciudad de México

North America

Canada

Greenland (Denmark)

United States of America

Belize

Honduras

Mexico

Costa Rica

Guatemala

El Salvador

Panama

Nicaragua

Caribbean Islands (political map)

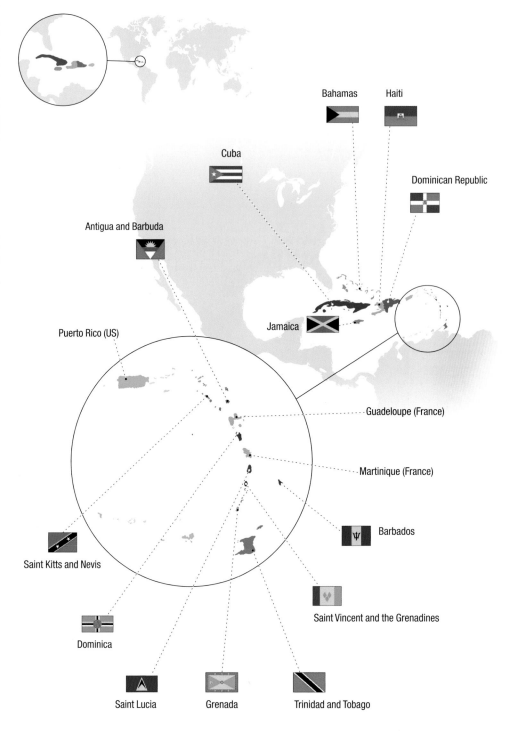

Bahamas

Haiti

Cuba

Dominican Republic

Antigua and Barbuda

Puerto Rico (US)

Jamaica

Guadeloupe (France)

Martinique (France)

Barbados

Saint Kitts and Nevis

Saint Vincent and the Grenadines

Dominica

Saint Lucia

Grenada

Trinidad and Tobago

South America (political map)

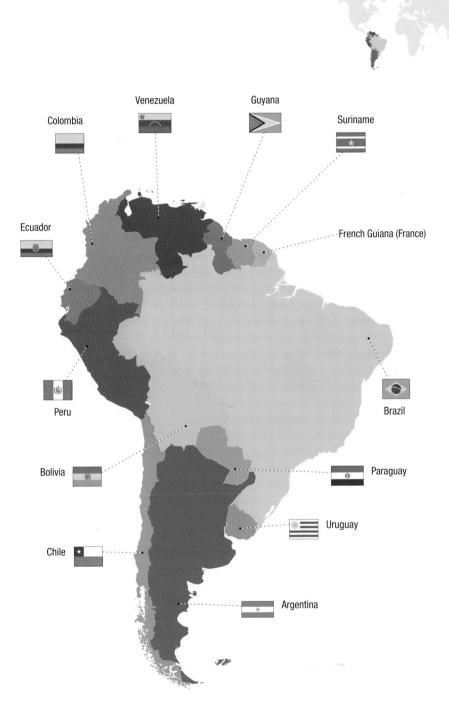

Colombia

Venezuela

Guyana

Suriname

Ecuador

French Guiana (France)

Peru

Brazil

Bolivia

Paraguay

Uruguay

Chile

Argentina

School

Europe (political map)

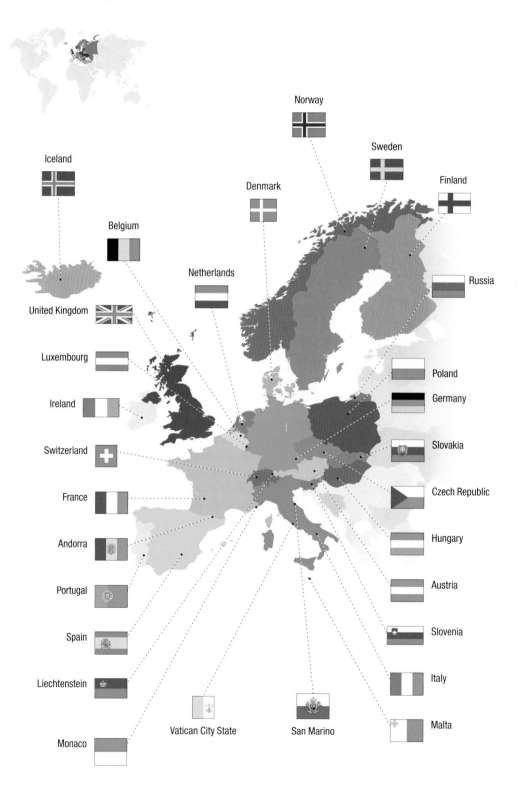

Norway

Iceland

Sweden

Denmark

Finland

Belgium

Netherlands

Russia

United Kingdom

Luxembourg

Poland

Ireland

Germany

Switzerland

Slovakia

France

Czech Republic

Andorra

Hungary

Portugal

Austria

Spain

Slovenia

Liechtenstein

Italy

Vatican City State

San Marino

Malta

Monaco

Europe (political map)

School

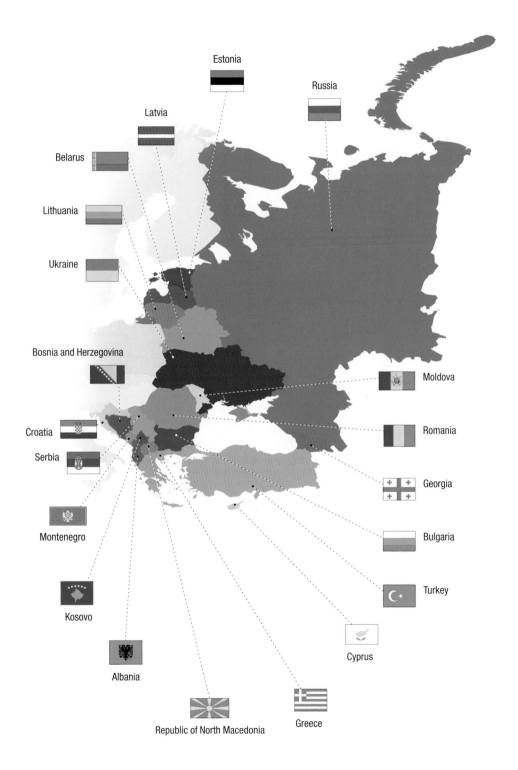

Estonia

Russia

Latvia

Belarus

Lithuania

Ukraine

Bosnia and Herzegovina

Moldova

Croatia

Romania

Serbia

Georgia

Montenegro

Bulgaria

Kosovo

Turkey

Cyprus

Albania

Republic of North Macedonia

Greece

Asia (political map)

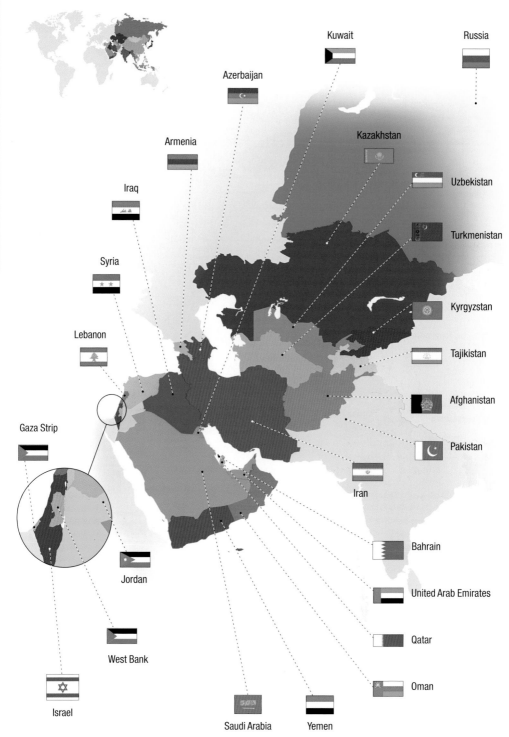

Kuwait

Russia

Azerbaijan

Kazakhstan

Armenia

Uzbekistan

Iraq

Turkmenistan

Syria

Kyrgyzstan

Lebanon

Tajikistan

Afghanistan

Gaza Strip

Pakistan

Iran

Bahrain

United Arab Emirates

Jordan

Qatar

West Bank

Oman

Israel

Saudi Arabia   Yemen

School

Asia (political map)

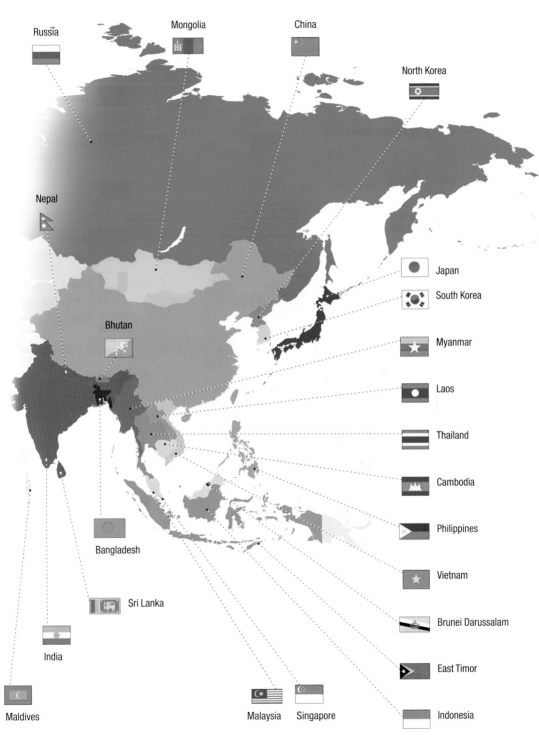

Russia

Mongolia

China

North Korea

Nepal

Japan

South Korea

Bhutan

Myanmar

Laos

Thailand

Cambodia

Philippines

Bangladesh

Vietnam

Sri Lanka

Brunei Darussalam

India

East Timor

Maldives

Malaysia   Singapore

Indonesia

Astronomy is the science of celestial bodies and the universe. The solar system is our little corner of the universe, in the Milky Way. It comprises one star (the Sun) and all the celestial bodies that orbit it: eight planets along with over a hundred natural satellites, hundreds of thousands of asteroids and possibly millions of comets. All kinds of inventions, including telescopes, have made it easier to observe all those bodies.

structure of the Sun

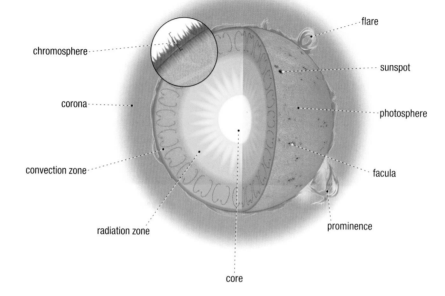

flare

chromosphere

sunspot

corona

photosphere

convection zone

facula

radiation zone

prominence

core

School

solar system

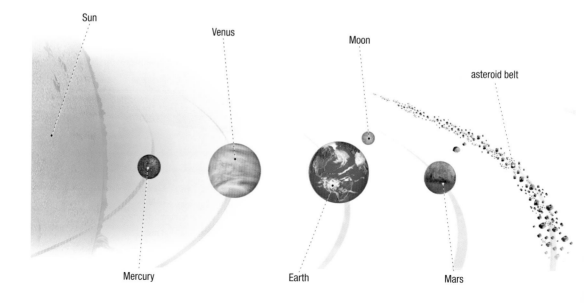

Sun

Venus

Moon

asteroid belt

Mercury

Earth

Mars

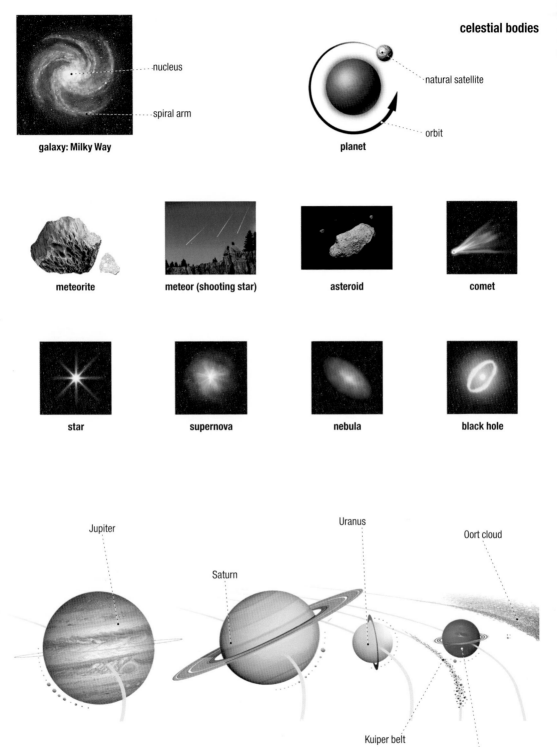

celestial bodies

nucleus

spiral arm

galaxy: Milky Way

natural satellite

orbit

planet

meteorite

meteor (shooting star)

asteroid

comet

star

supernova

nebula

black hole

School

Jupiter

Saturn

Uranus

Oort cloud

Kuiper belt

Neptune

School

eclipses

solar eclipse

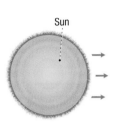
Sun

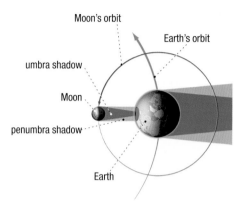
Moon's orbit
Earth's orbit
umbra shadow
Moon
penumbra shadow
Earth

partial solar eclipse

total solar eclipse

lunar eclipse

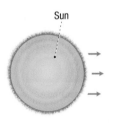
Sun

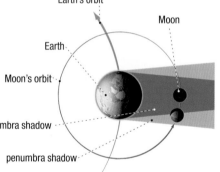
Earth's orbit
Moon
Earth
Moon's orbit
umbra shadow
penumbra shadow

partial lunar eclipse

total lunar eclipse

phases of the Moon

new moon

new crescent

first quarter

waxing gibbous

full moon

waning gibbous

last quarter

old crescent

astronomical observation

refracting telescope

reflecting telescope

radio telescope

astronomical observatory

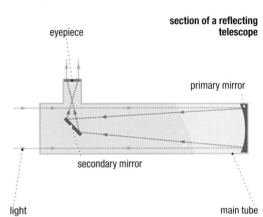

section of a reflecting telescope

eyepiece

primary mirror

secondary mirror

light

main tube

space exploration

spacesuit

spaceship

space probe

international space station

universe
solar storm
stargazing
meteor shower
binoculars
astronomer
astronaut
light-year
crescent moon
gravity
weightlessness
star chart
planetarium
to be in orbit

payload

liquid oxygen tank

liquid hydrogen tank

solid rocket booster

nozzle

rocket engine

space launcher

Physics focuses on forces, movements and the different kinds of energy that shape the universe. The things that physicists analyze, like gravity, light and sound, have led to the invention of the technology that makes our everyday lives better. That includes all devices powered by waves, electricity, electronics or simple mechanical movements.

physics: mechanics

lever

School

double pulley system

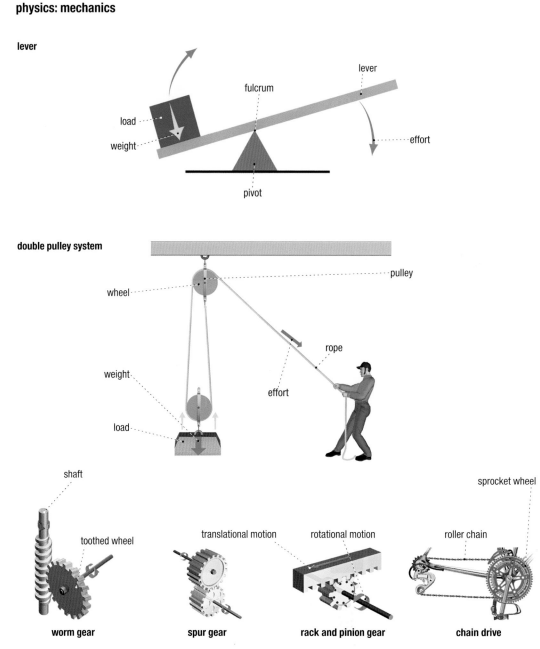

worm gear   spur gear   rack and pinion gear   chain drive

physics: optics

wave

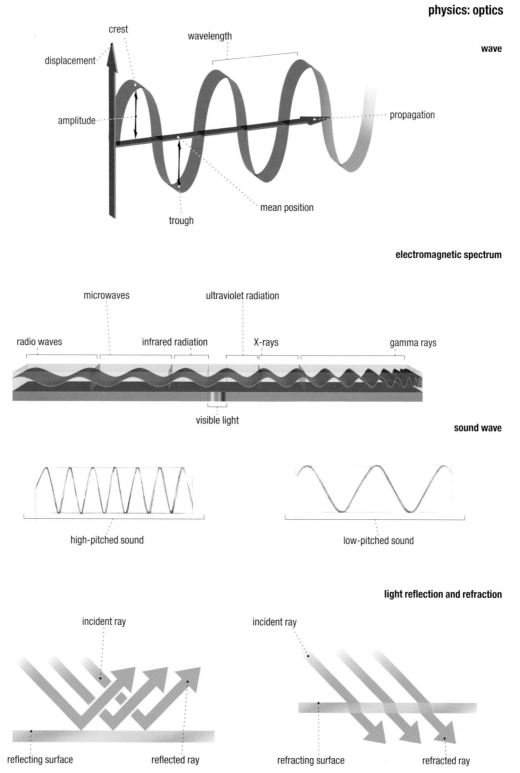

crest

wavelength

displacement

amplitude

propagation

mean position

trough

electromagnetic spectrum

microwaves

ultraviolet radiation

radio waves

infrared radiation

X-rays

gamma rays

visible light

sound wave

high-pitched sound

low-pitched sound

light reflection and refraction

incident ray

incident ray

reflecting surface

reflected ray

refracting surface

refracted ray

School

optical devices (reflection)

mirror

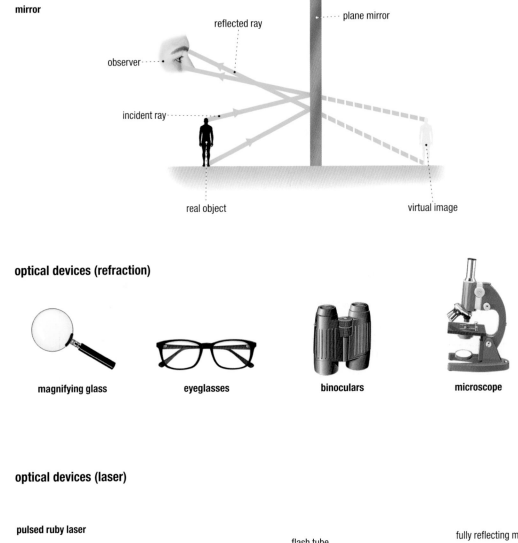

observer · · · ·

reflected ray

plane mirror

incident ray · · · ·

real object

virtual image

optical devices (refraction)

magnifying glass **eyeglasses** **binoculars** **microscope**

optical devices (laser)

pulsed ruby laser

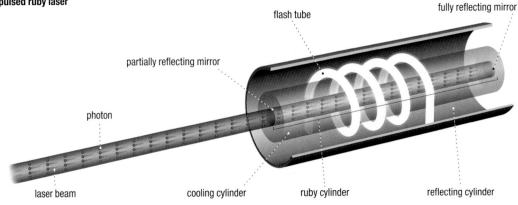

flash tube

fully reflecting mirror

partially reflecting mirror

photon

laser beam cooling cylinder ruby cylinder reflecting cylinder

physics: electricity and magnetism

magnet

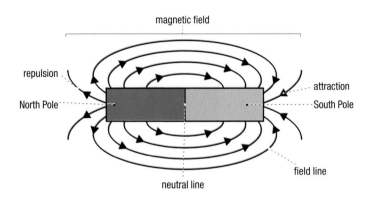

magnetic field

repulsion

North Pole

attraction

South Pole

field line

neutral line

dry cell: manganese-zinc

Earth's magnetic field

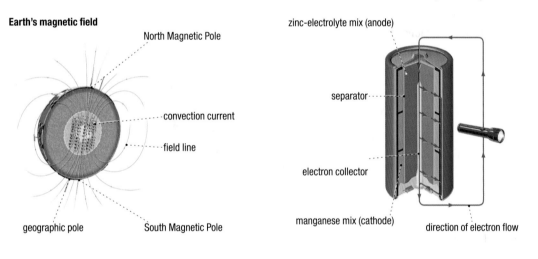

North Magnetic Pole

zinc-electrolyte mix (anode)

convection current

separator

field line

electron collector

geographic pole

South Magnetic Pole

manganese mix (cathode)

direction of electron flow

electrical circuit

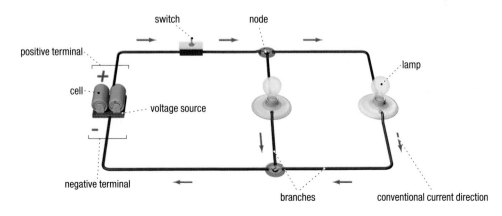

switch

node

positive terminal

lamp

cell

voltage source

negative terminal

branches

conventional current direction

renewable energies

hydroelectricity

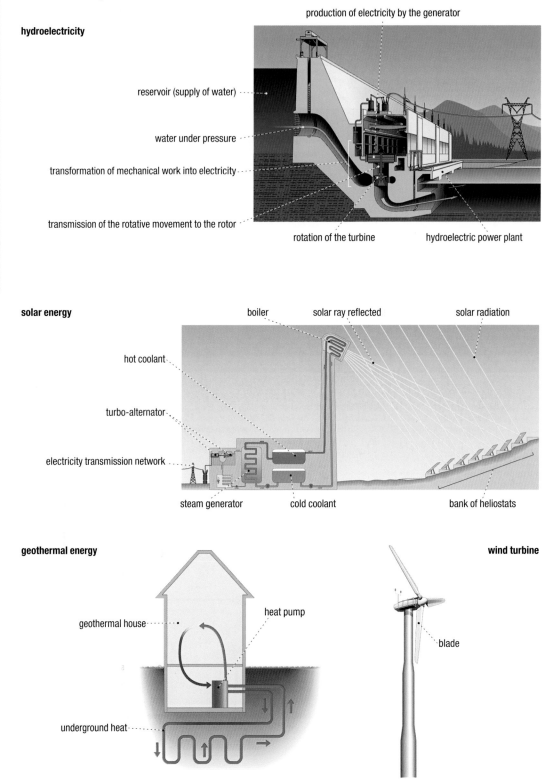

production of electricity by the generator

reservoir (supply of water)

water under pressure

transformation of mechanical work into electricity

transmission of the rotative movement to the rotor

rotation of the turbine

hydroelectric power plant

solar energy

boiler

solar ray reflected

solar radiation

hot coolant

turbo-alternator

electricity transmission network

steam generator

cold coolant

bank of heliostats

geothermal energy

wind turbine

heat pump

geothermal house

blade

underground heat

non-renewable energy

nuclear energy

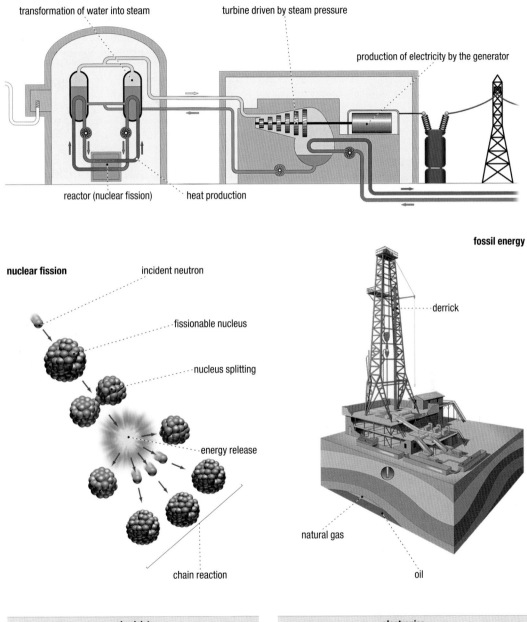

transformation of water into steam

turbine driven by steam pressure

production of electricity by the generator

reactor (nuclear fission)

heat production

nuclear fission

incident neutron

fissionable nucleus

nucleus splitting

energy release

chain reaction

fossil energy

derrick

natural gas

oil

School

physicist	electronics
gravity	integrated circuit
speed of light	printed circuit
resonance	energy consumption
frequency	coal
electromagnetism	biodiesel
static electricity	biofuel

chronology of discoveries and inventions

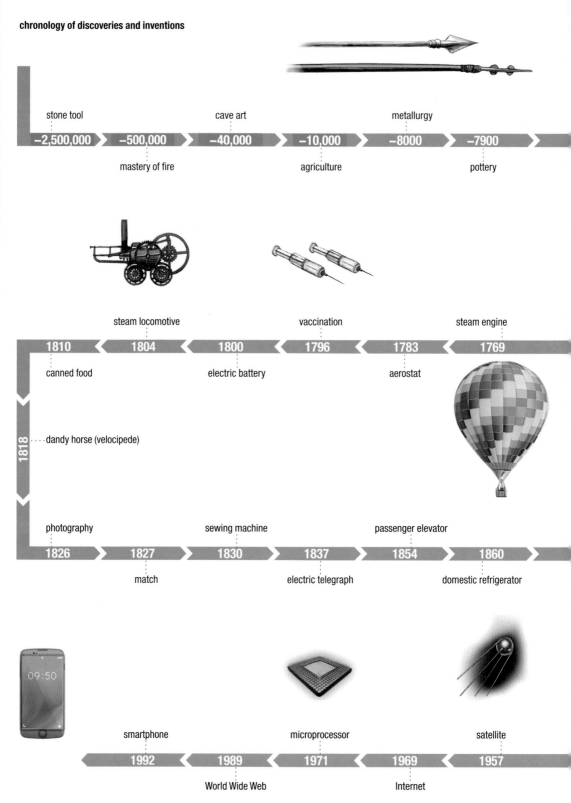

stone tool
cave art
metallurgy

| −2,500,000 | −500,000 | −40,000 | −10,000 | −8000 | −7900 |

mastery of fire
agriculture
pottery

steam locomotive
vaccination
steam engine

| 1810 | 1804 | 1800 | 1796 | 1783 | 1769 |

canned food
electric battery
aerostat

1818 · · · · dandy horse (velocipede)

photography
sewing machine
passenger elevator

| 1826 | 1827 | 1830 | 1837 | 1854 | 1860 |

match
electric telegraph
domestic refrigerator

smartphone
microprocessor
satellite

| 1992 | 1989 | 1971 | 1969 | 1957 |

World Wide Web
Internet

School

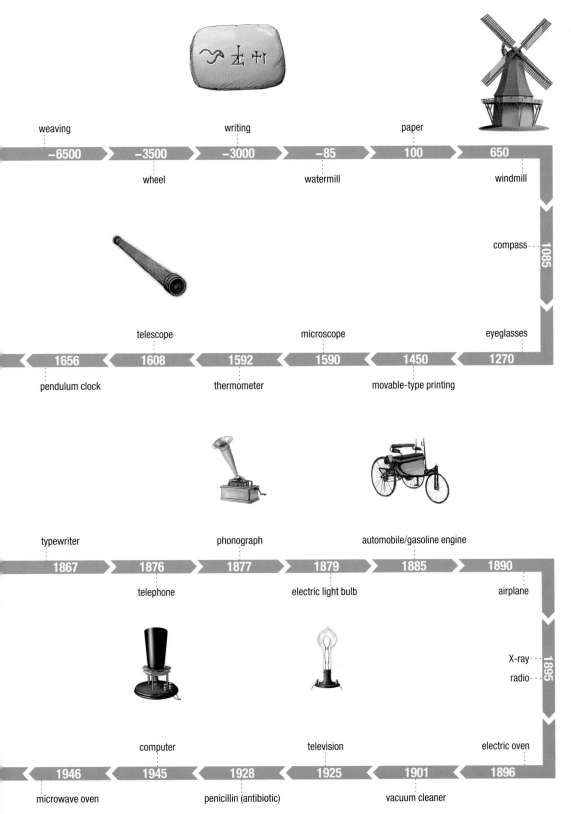

weaving
| −6500 | −3500 | −3000 | −85 | 100 | 650 |
wheel   watermill   windmill
writing   paper

compass

1085

telescope   microscope   eyeglasses
| 1656 | 1608 | 1592 | 1590 | 1450 | 1270 |
pendulum clock   thermometer   movable-type printing

typewriter   phonograph   automobile/gasoline engine
| 1867 | 1876 | 1877 | 1879 | 1885 | 1890 |
telephone   electric light bulb   airplane

X-ray
radio

1895

computer   television   electric oven
| 1946 | 1945 | 1928 | 1925 | 1901 | 1896 |
microwave oven   penicillin (antibiotic)   vacuum cleaner

School

Mathematics deals with numbers. It is used for solving problems and establishing formulas to represent the theories governing the universe. By way of example, we can use mathematics to predict tomorrow's weather or calculate a planet's trajectory. The science of mathematics underlies all scientific domains, but it is also very useful in everyday life.

geometry: circle and angles

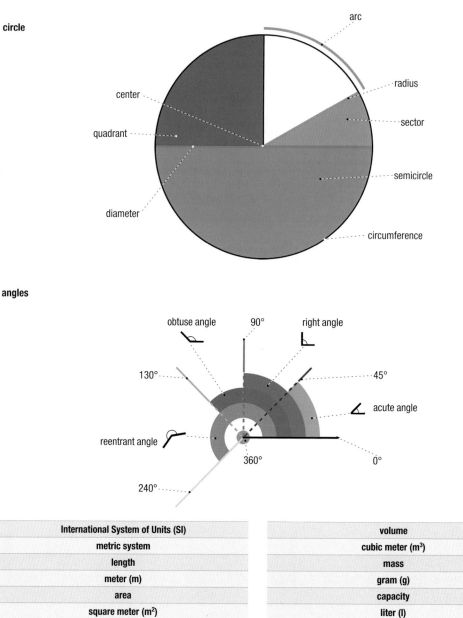

circle

arc

radius

center

sector

quadrant

semicircle

diameter

circumference

angles

obtuse angle   90°   right angle

130°   45°

acute angle

reentrant angle

360°   0°

240°

International System of Units (SI)	volume
metric system	cubic meter (m³)
length	mass
meter (m)	gram (g)
area	capacity
square meter (m²)	liter (l)

School

geometry: polygons

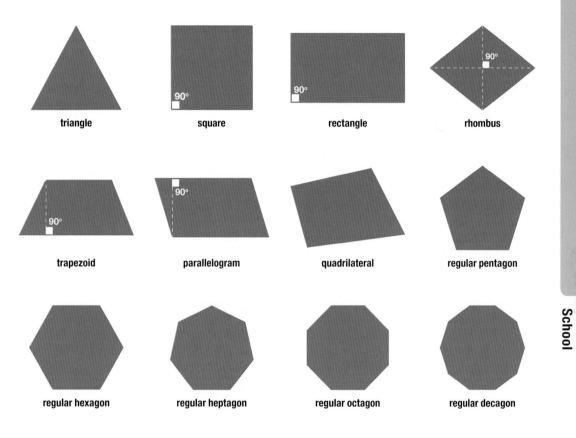

triangle

square

rectangle

rhombus

trapezoid

parallelogram

quadrilateral

regular pentagon

regular hexagon

regular heptagon

regular octagon

regular decagon

geometry: solids

sphere

cylinder

cube

pyramid

cone

rectangular prism

triangular prism

statistics

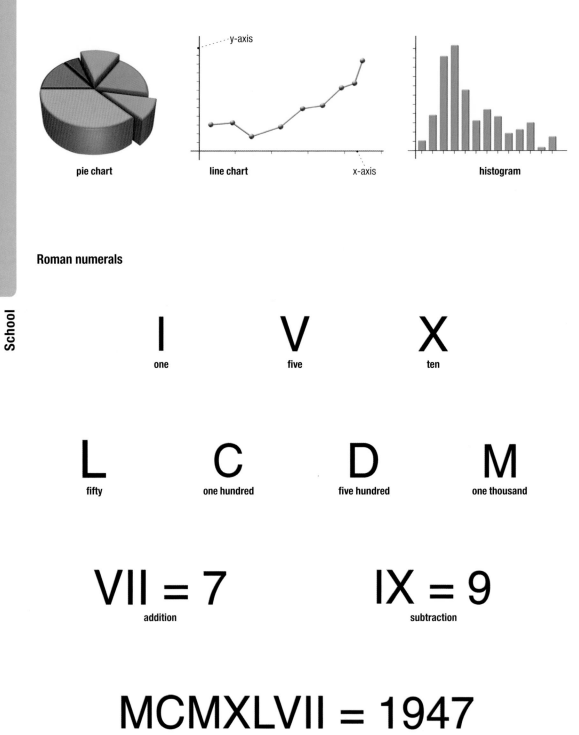

pie chart · line chart · y-axis · x-axis · histogram

Roman numerals

I
one

V
five

X
ten

L
fifty

C
one hundred

D
five hundred

M
one thousand

VII = 7
addition

IX = 9
subtraction

MCMXLVII = 1947
synthesis

symbols

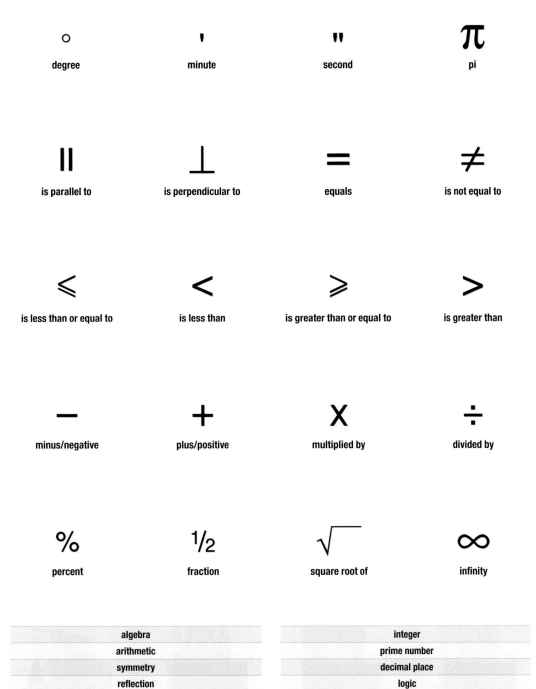

○	'	"	π
degree	minute	second	pi
‖	⊥	=	≠
is parallel to	is perpendicular to	equals	is not equal to
⩽	<	⩾	>
is less than or equal to	is less than	is greater than or equal to	is greater than
—	+	X	÷
minus/negative	plus/positive	multiplied by	divided by
%	½	√	∞
percent	fraction	square root of	infinity

School

algebra	integer
arithmetic	prime number
symmetry	decimal place
reflection	logic
rotation	to calculate
translation	to measure
equation	to estimate
formula	to solve

wood carving

drawing

roughing out

carving

finishing

chisel

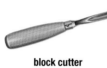

block cutter

gouge

knife

graphic arts

engraving

ink

brayer

proof press

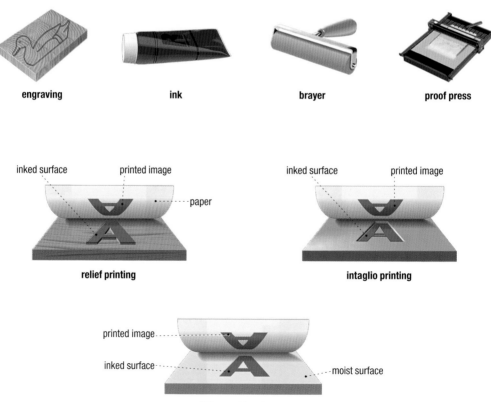

inked surface — printed image — paper

relief printing

inked surface — printed image

intaglio printing

printed image — inked surface — moist surface

lithographic printing

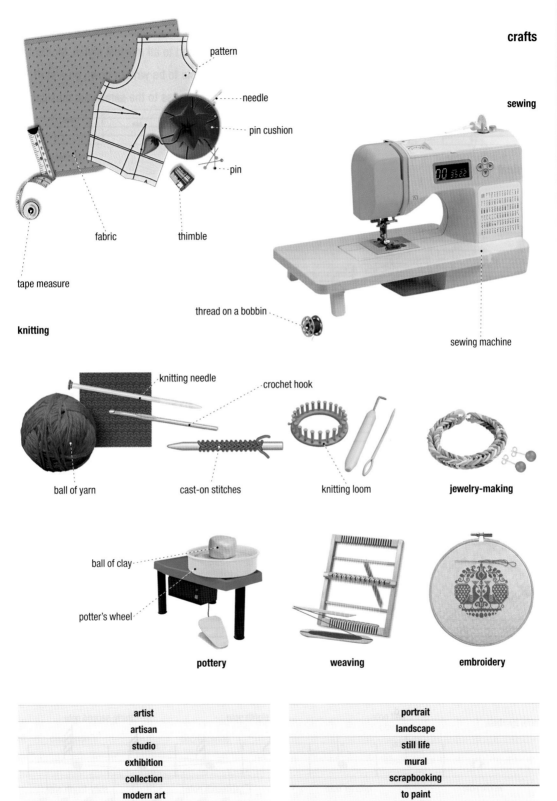

crafts

pattern

needle

pin cushion

pin

sewing

fabric

thimble

tape measure

thread on a bobbin

sewing machine

knitting

knitting needle

crochet hook

ball of yarn

cast-on stitches

knitting loom

jewelry-making

ball of clay

potter's wheel

pottery

weaving

embroidery

School

artist	portrait
artisan	landscape
studio	still life
exhibition	mural
collection	scrapbooking
modern art	to paint
contemporary art	to create

School

stringed instruments

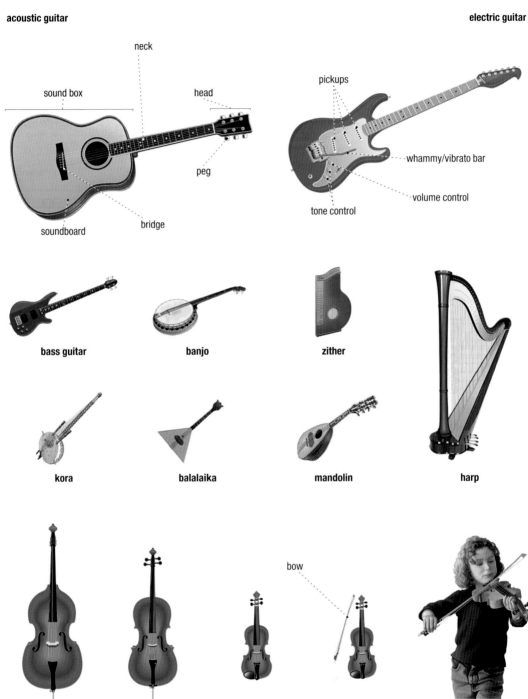

acoustic guitar

electric guitar

neck

sound box

head

pickups

peg

whammy/vibrato bar

volume control

tone control

soundboard

bridge

bass guitar

banjo

zither

kora

balalaika

mandolin

harp

bow

double bass

cello

viola

violin

violinist

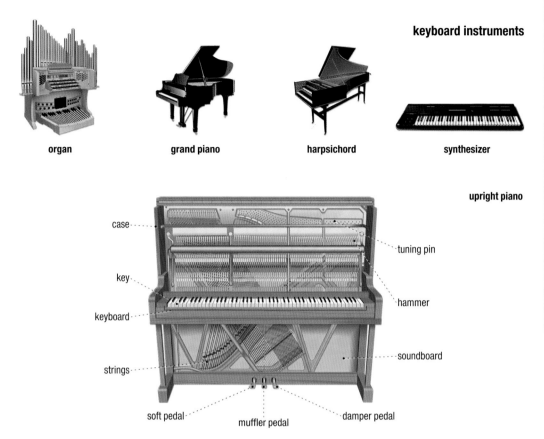

keyboard instruments

organ

grand piano

harpsichord

synthesizer

upright piano

case

tuning pin

key

hammer

keyboard

soundboard

strings

soft pedal

muffler pedal

damper pedal

percussion instruments

mallets

drum kit

tom-tom

cymbal

drumsticks

xylophone

tambourine

snare drum

djembe

bongos

bass drum

tenor drum

All the different architectural styles are a reflection of world history and past civilizations. Many events have shaped today's world and society—natural disasters, migrations, discoveries, technological and social revolutions, and wars. As different people come together they spark changes that give rise to new civilizations.

ancient architecture

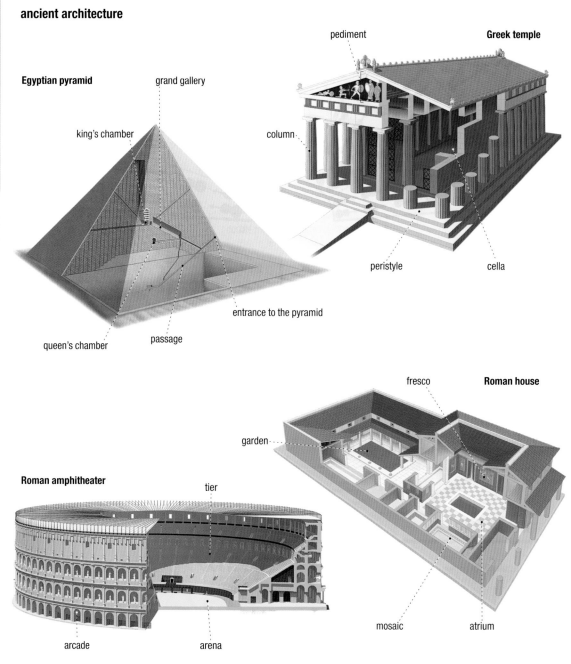

Egyptian pyramid

grand gallery

king's chamber

queen's chamber

passage

entrance to the pyramid

Greek temple

pediment

column

peristyle

cella

Roman house

fresco

garden

mosaic

atrium

Roman amphitheater

tier

arcade

arena

School

medieval architecture

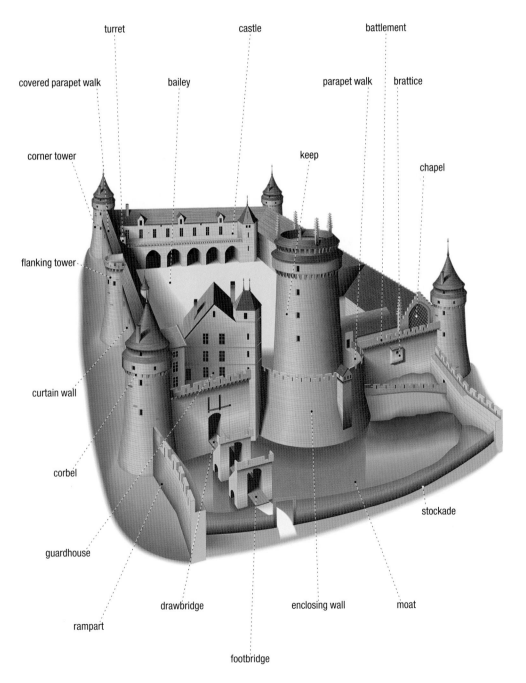

turret

castle

battlement

covered parapet walk

bailey

parapet walk

brattice

corner tower

keep

chapel

flanking tower

curtain wall

corbel

guardhouse

stockade

rampart

drawbridge

enclosing wall

moat

footbridge

School

medieval architecture

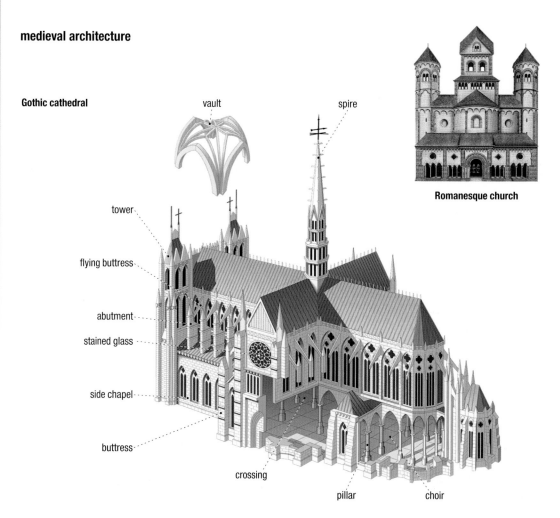

Gothic cathedral

vault

spire

Romanesque church

tower

flying buttress

abutment

stained glass

side chapel

buttress

crossing

pillar

choir

Asian and pre-Columbian architecture

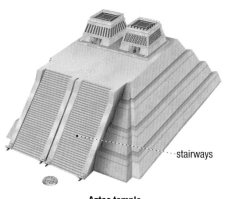

stairways

Aztec temple

finial

roof

balustrade

pillar

podium

pagoda

examples of architectural styles

classical/neoclassical style

baroque/rococo

Islamic style

art nouveau

art deco

expressionism

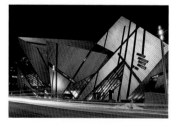
international style

constructivism

deconstructivism

School

migration	colonization
settlement	decolonization
civilization	nationalism
citizenship	independence
democracy	revolution
imperialism	aboriginal
monarchy	emigrant
dictatorship	immigrant
war	remains
invasion	monument
capitalism	tomb
socialism	archaeology
communism	anthropology
social class	historian

timeline

−300,000	−120,000	−50,000
emergence of *Homo sapiens* in Africa	beginning of migrations towards Eurasia	arrival of *Homo sapiens* in Australia

−776	−1000	−1750
first Olympic Games (Greece)	colonization of Pacific islands	Code of Hammurabi (Mesopotamia)

−507	−331	−322
first democracy (Athens, Greece)	founding of Alexandria (Egypt)	beginning of the Maurya Empire (India)

800	762	622
Charlemagne crowned emperor (Europe)	founding of Baghdad (Middle East)	start of Islamic conquests (Asia, Africa)

868	962	1096
first known printed book (China)	beginning of the Holy Germanic Empire	start of the Crusades (Europe, Near East)

1494	1492	1455
Spain and Portugal share control of the New World	arrival of Christopher Columbus in the Americas	invention and spread of the printing press

1522	1533	1543
Spanish expedition completes the first circumnavigation of the earth	end of pre-Columbian civilizations (Americas)	Nicolaus Copernicus' heliocentric theory

School

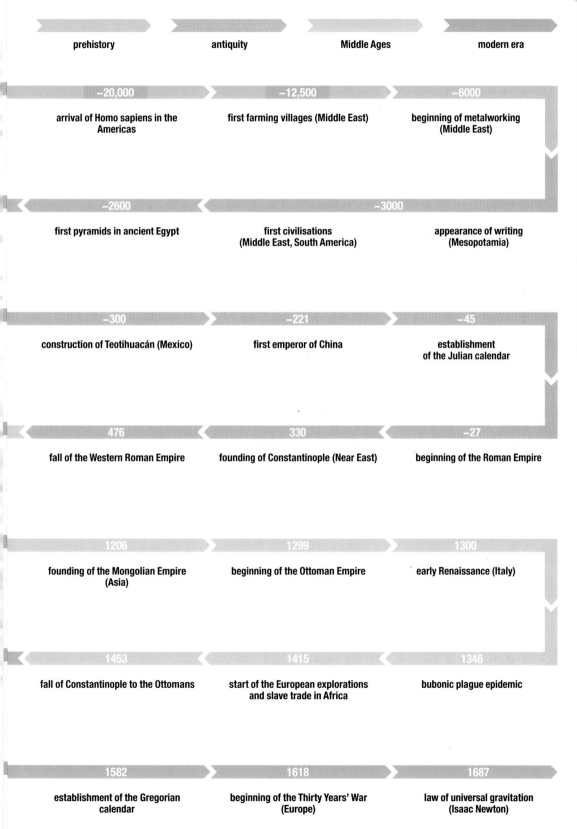

prehistory

antiquity

Middle Ages

modern era

−20,000	−12,500	−6000
arrival of Homo sapiens in the Americas	first farming villages (Middle East)	beginning of metalworking (Middle East)

−2600	−3000	
first pyramids in ancient Egypt	first civilisations (Middle East, South America)	appearance of writing (Mesopotamia)

−300	−221	−45
construction of Teotihuacán (Mexico)	first emperor of China	establishment of the Julian calendar

476	330	−27
fall of the Western Roman Empire	founding of Constantinople (Near East)	beginning of the Roman Empire

1206	1299	1300
founding of the Mongolian Empire (Asia)	beginning of the Ottoman Empire	early Renaissance (Italy)

1453	1415	1346
fall of Constantinople to the Ottomans	start of the European explorations and slave trade in Africa	bubonic plague epidemic

1582	1618	1687
establishment of the Gregorian calendar	beginning of the Thirty Years' War (Europe)	law of universal gravitation (Isaac Newton)

School

What we learn in school not only builds our general knowledge but prepares us for more specialized studies and future jobs. Some professions like medicine or law require advanced degrees. People can go to trade schools to become electricians or mechanics. Choosing training in line with our interests and aptitudes will allow us to enjoy our future employment.

higher education and specialization

········campus

college/university

·····apprentice

·····master

trade school

········professor

········student

classroom

academy

training course

dormitory

scholarship

·· employer

·· job applicant

job interview
·résumé

graduation ceremony

seasonal work

diploma
medicine
law
political science
economics
humanities
social science
engineering
master's degree
doctorate (PhD)
ability/aptitude
to learn a trade/skill
to apply for a job

part-time work

full-time work

Work

examples of occupations

police officer

security guard

soldier

firefighter

farmer

mechanic

pilot

flight attendant

driver

cleaner

salesperson

store clerk

hair stylist

waiter/waitress

cook/chef

construction worker

plumber

electrician

Work

office

office organization

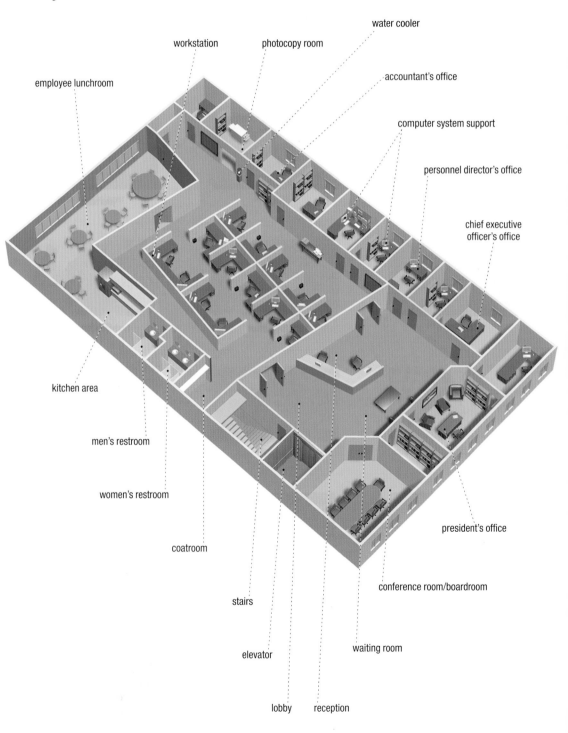

water cooler

workstation

photocopy room

accountant's office

employee lunchroom

computer system support

personnel director's office

chief executive officer's office

kitchen area

men's restroom

women's restroom

coatroom

president's office

stairs

conference room/boardroom

elevator

waiting room

lobby   reception

office furniture and stationery

workstation

computer

telephone

desk

drawer

pull-out keyboard shelf

printer table

keyboard

footrest

office chair

wastebasket

folder

carry folder

memo pad

pen

stapler

staple remover

document handler

photocopier

staples

paper clips

feeder output tray

bypass feeder

paper trays

Work

company	**leave**
management	**pay/salary**
manager	**deduction/tax**
staff	**layoff**
customer/client	**unemployment**
meeting	**to have an appointment**
union	**to serve a client**

Vacation

People often choose coastal regions for vacation destinations. The beauty and natural setting is enticing during the warmer months. Beaches offer varied recreational and leisure activities for every vacationer.

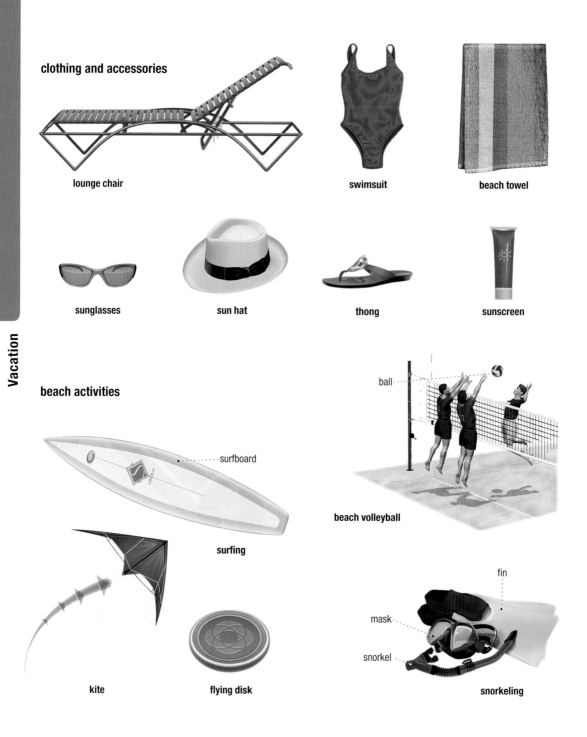

clothing and accessories

lounge chair

swimsuit

beach towel

sunglasses

sun hat

thong

sunscreen

beach activities

surfboard

surfing

ball

beach volleyball

kite

flying disk

fin

mask

snorkel

snorkeling

marine life

coral reef

fish

seashells

dolphin

seaweed

jellyfish

gull

crab

beach

Vacation

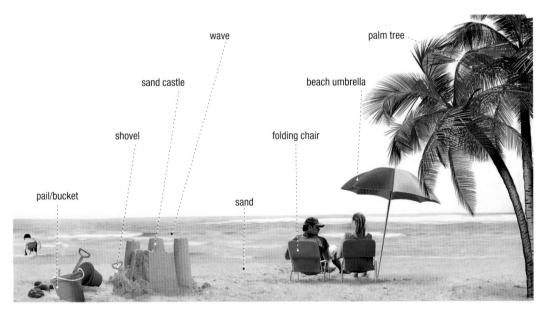

wave

sand castle

palm tree

beach umbrella

shovel

folding chair

pail/bucket

sand

lifeguard	cooler
life buoy	after-sun cream
high/low tide	in the sun/shade
current	to tan
calm/rough sea	to get sunburned
beach hut	to put on sunscreen
boardwalk	No swimming!

Waterways, which used to be so crucial for long journeys, are today crisscrossed by pleasure boats—some of which are propelled by paddles or sails. Fishing is a popular sport as well as a commercial activity. Whatever you do on or in the water, be sure to follow all safety rules.

pleasure craft and water sports

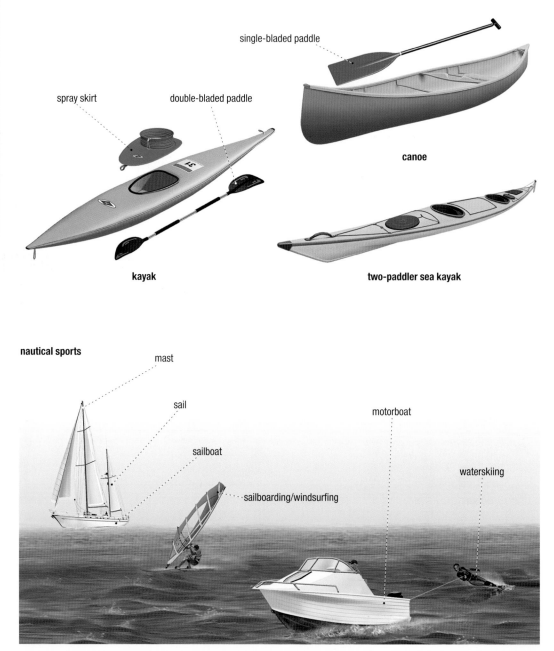

single-bladed paddle

spray skirt   double-bladed paddle

canoe

kayak

two-paddler sea kayak

nautical sports

mast

sail

motorboat

sailboat

waterskiing

sailboarding/windsurfing

Vacation

nautical safety

distress beacon   boat hook   life buoy   life jacket/life vest

fishing

fishing rod

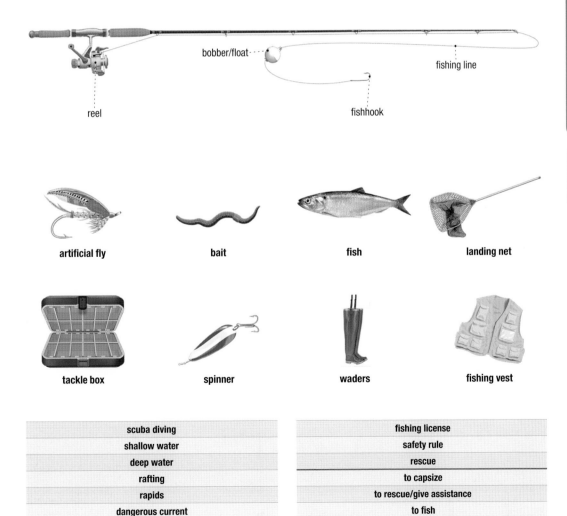

bobber/float

fishing line

reel

fishhook

artificial fly   bait   fish   landing net

tackle box   spinner   waders   fishing vest

Vacation

scuba diving	fishing license
shallow water	safety rule
deep water	rescue
rafting	to capsize
rapids	to rescue/give assistance
dangerous current	to fish
wind direction	Help!

Camping is ideal as an inexpensive, open-air way to travel. At the very least, all you need is a sleeping bag and a few utensils, but you will be more comfortable if you also have a tent and a mattress, among other things. Camping and hiking are ways to enjoy the beauty of nature, which is ours to take care of.

Vacation

camping

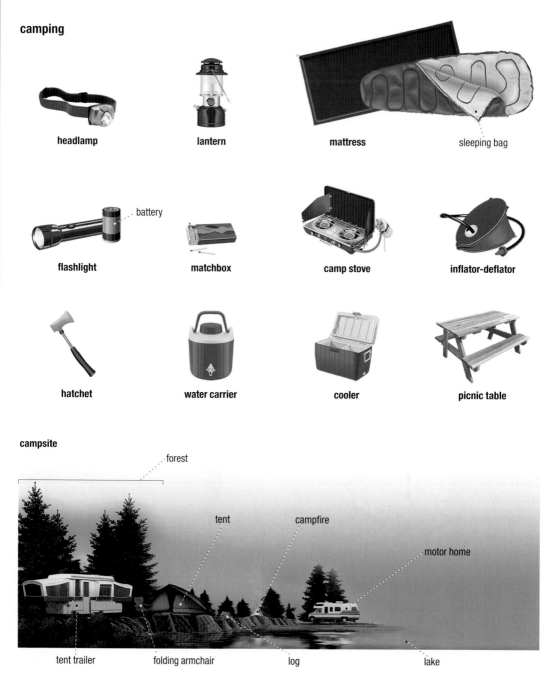

headlamp

lantern

mattress

sleeping bag

flashlight — battery

matchbox

camp stove

inflator-deflator

hatchet

water carrier

cooler

picnic table

campsite

forest

tent

campfire

motor home

tent trailer

folding armchair

log

lake

hiking

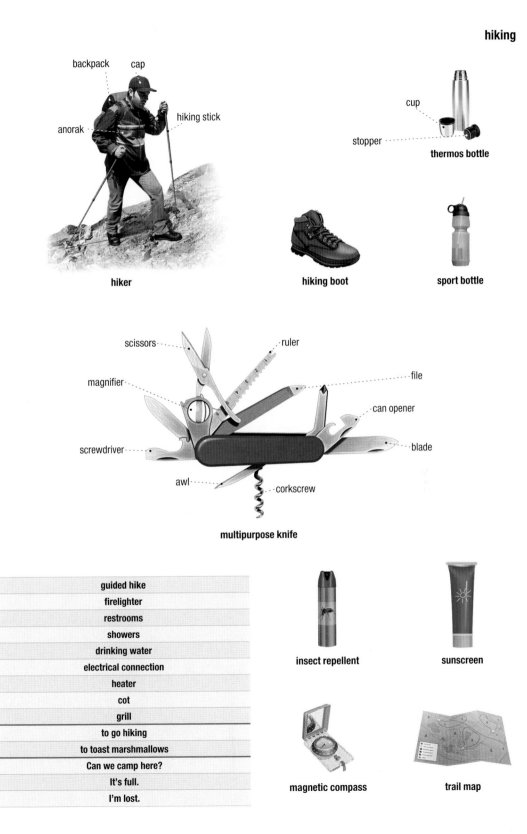

backpack
cap
anorak
hiking stick

hiker

cup
stopper
thermos bottle

hiking boot

sport bottle

scissors
ruler
magnifier
file
can opener
screwdriver
blade
awl
corkscrew

multipurpose knife

guided hike
firelighter
restrooms
showers
drinking water
electrical connection
heater
cot
grill
to go hiking
to toast marshmallows
Can we camp here?
It's full.
I'm lost.

insect repellent

sunscreen

magnetic compass

trail map

Vacation

We go to the country to breathe fresh air and get away from the busy city. Wide-open spaces are also good for farming and producing the food we need to eat. Furthermore, the countryside is a great place for recreational activities like hiking and horseback riding

farmstead

meadow

barn

machinery shed

stable

fallow

tower silo

feed corn

permanent pasture

fence

vegetable garden

cowshed

farmhouse

sheep shelter

henhouse

enclosure

greenhouse

pigpen

fruit tree   hive   orchard

fitness equipment

home gym

stationary bicycle

treadmill

chest expander

weight

dumbbells

jump rope

exercise mat

fitness ball

fitness

aerobics

Pilates

jogging

swimming

push-up

sit-up

weight training

stretching

training	muscle strengthening
training room	walking
trainer	running
warm-up	yoga
squat	relaxation
muscle tone	to train
ache	to be in good/poor shape
muscle strain	

Sports

Gymnastics and athletics include events demanding agility, strength and flexibility all at the same time. Some athletic events like running, long jump, javelin and discus have a long history. They were featured at the very first Olympic Games in Ancient Greece.

Sports

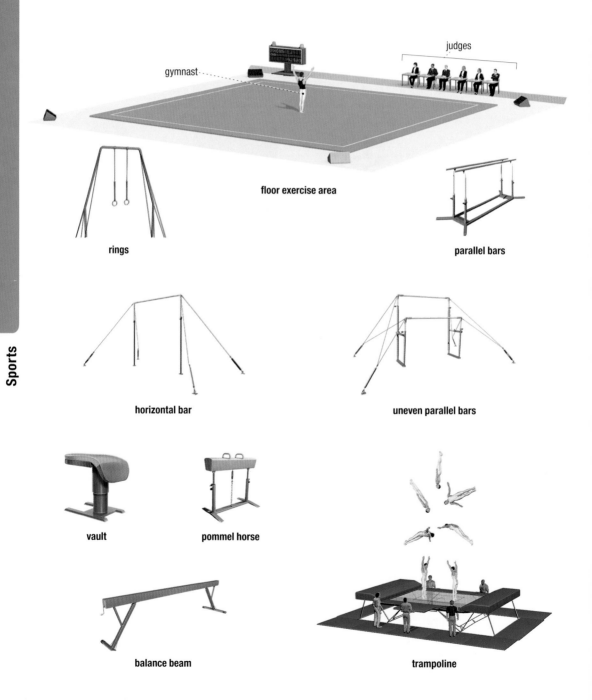

judges

gymnast

floor exercise area

rings

parallel bars

horizontal bar

uneven parallel bars

vault

pommel horse

balance beam

trampoline

running

runner

arena

starting block

track

lane

finish line

sprint

number

marathon

baton

relay

hurdle

high jump

long jump

pole vault

Sports

javelin throw

shot put

discus throw

hammer throw

event
endurance
triathlon
gold/silver/bronze medal
record
to win an event

cross-country running

Ball sports are mainly played in teams. In baseball, field hockey, soccer, football, basketball and volleyball, the players have to follow the rules of the game while trying to outplay their opponents. Many ball sports are played on fields or courts that are either indoors or outdoors.

basketball

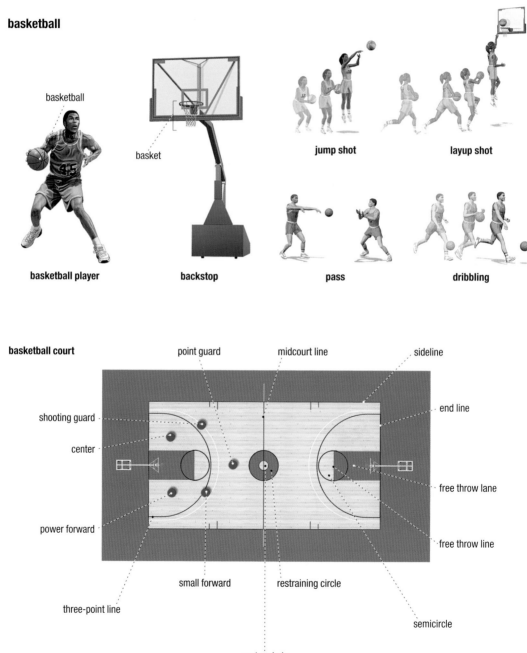

basketball

jump shot   **layup shot**

basketball player   **backstop**   **pass**   **dribbling**

basket

basketball court

point guard   midcourt line   sideline

shooting guard   end line

center

power forward   free throw lane

free throw line

three-point line   small forward   restraining circle   semicircle

center circle

Sports

soccer player

soccer

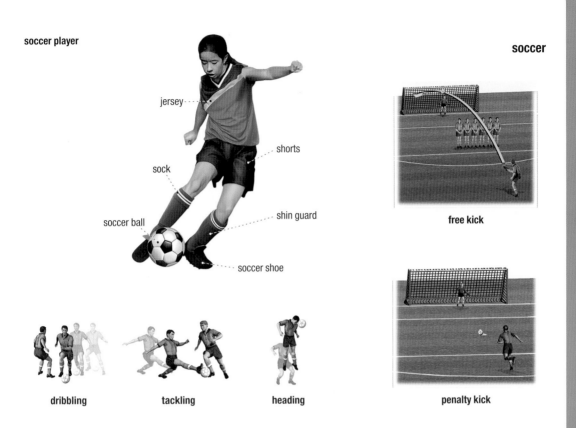

jersey

shorts

sock

shin guard

soccer ball

soccer shoe

free kick

dribbling

tackling

heading

penalty kick

soccer field

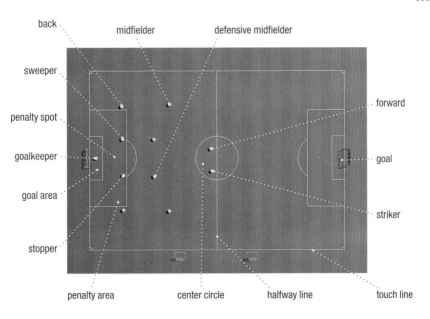

back

midfielder

defensive midfielder

sweeper

forward

penalty spot

goalkeeper

goal

goal area

stopper

striker

penalty area

center circle

halfway line

touch line

volleyball

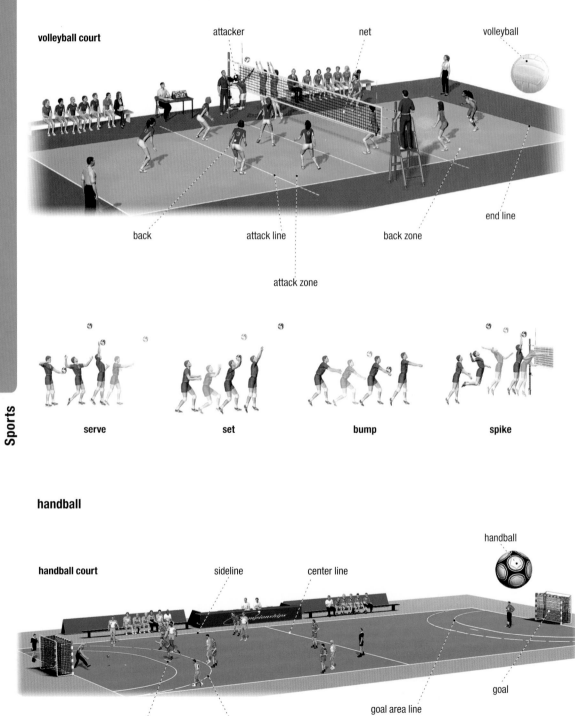

volleyball court   attacker   net   volleyball

end line

back   attack line   back zone

attack zone

serve   **set**   **bump**   **spike**

handball

handball   handball court   sideline   center line

goal

goal area line

penalty mark   free throw line

catcher   batter   home plate   pitcher   **baseball**

baseball

baseball glove

baseball bat

helmet

football

cleated shoe

football

stick

hockey ball

field hockey

bat

cricket ball

cricket

rugby ball

scrum   **rugby**

Sports

game	overtime
player	tie game
team	qualifying
score	tournament
umpire/referee	whistle
coach	foul
fan	ejection
club	to catch
offside	to block
period	to score a goal/run/touchdown

Tennis is the most popular racket sport. It is a game for two or four players played on clay, grass or hard courts around the world. Tennis players hit a ball across a net at speeds that can top 124 miles (200 kilometers) per hour. Several major tournaments attract thousands of spectators every year; Wimbledon in England is the oldest and the most famous.

Sports

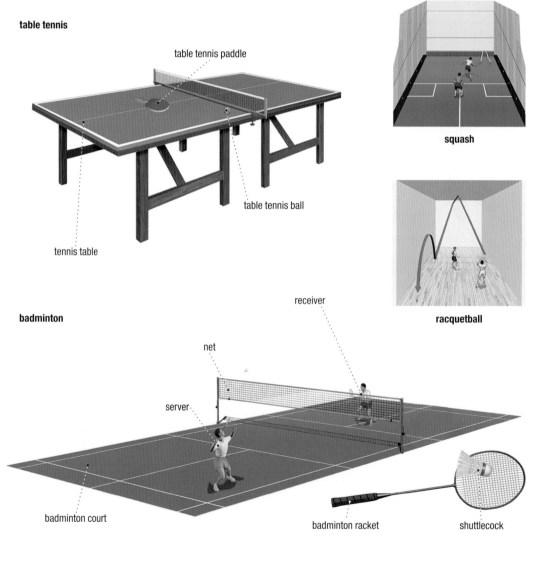

table tennis

table tennis paddle

table tennis ball

tennis table

squash

racquetball

badminton

receiver

net

server

badminton court

badminton racket

shuttlecock

set	ace
game	backhand
point	forehand
advantage	fault
deuce	singles
tie-breaker	doubles
rally	mixed doubles

tennis

tennis court

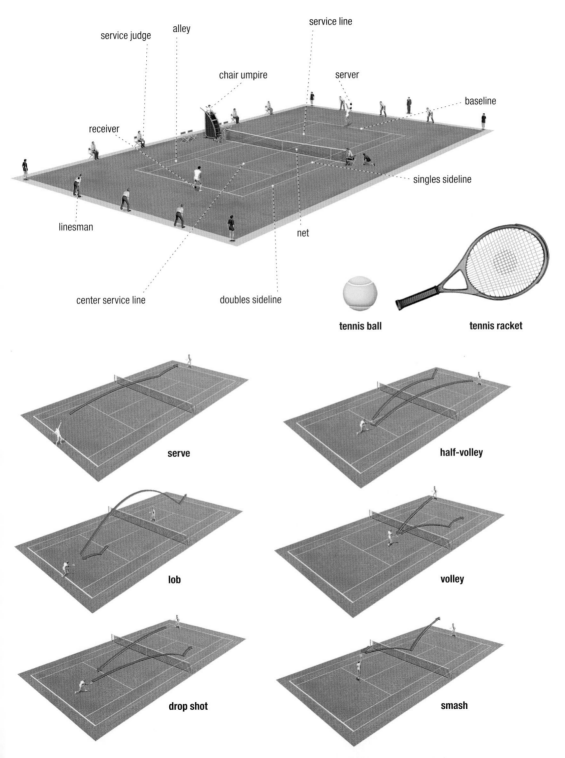

service judge

alley

service line

chair umpire

server

baseline

receiver

singles sideline

linesman

net

center service line

doubles sideline

tennis ball

tennis racket

serve

half-volley

lob

volley

drop shot

smash

A swimmer's main goal is to glide through the water as quickly as possible with the least amount of effort. In order to do that, swimmers have to perfect their techniques by training intensively and constantly. They usually specialize in one of the four recognized styles: front crawl, breaststroke, butterfly and backstroke.

Sports

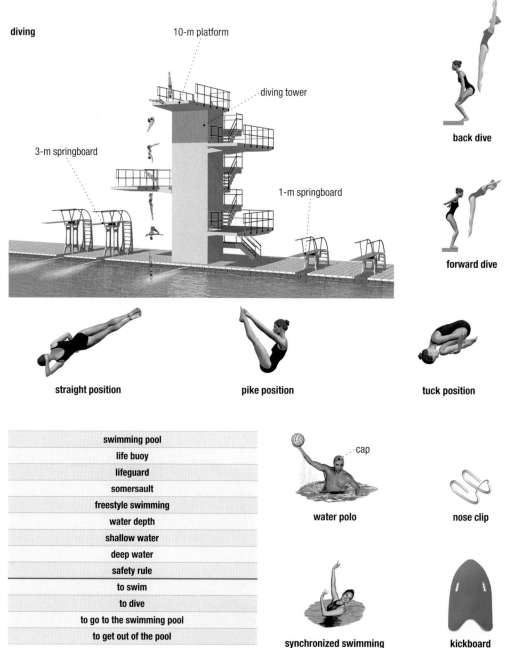

diving

10-m platform

diving tower

3-m springboard

1-m springboard

back dive

forward dive

straight position

pike position

tuck position

swimming pool
life buoy
lifeguard
somersault
freestyle swimming
water depth
shallow water
deep water
safety rule
to swim
to dive
to go to the swimming pool
to get out of the pool

cap

water polo

nose clip

synchronized swimming

kickboard

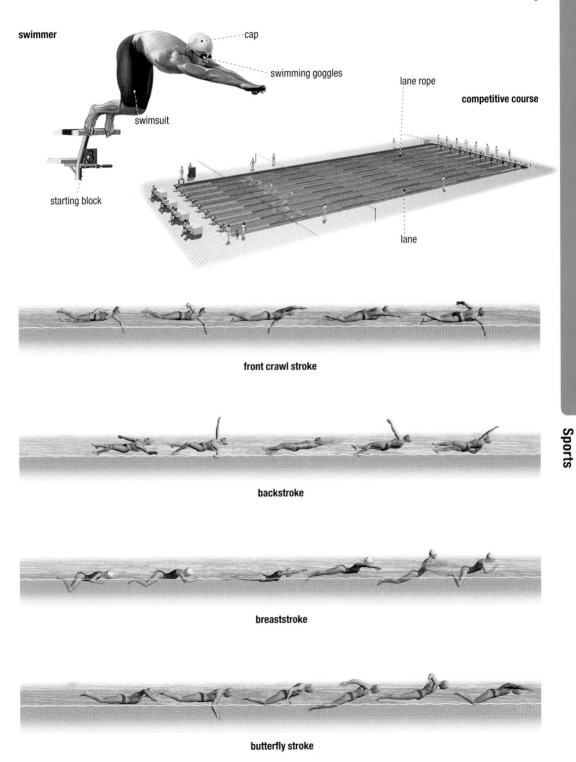

swimming

swimmer

cap

swimming goggles

swimsuit

starting block

lane rope

competitive course

lane

front crawl stroke

backstroke

breaststroke

butterfly stroke

As the name suggests, precision and accuracy sports require a perfect mastery of one's movements and a high level of concentration. Whether the athlete is shooting an arrow, sliding a curling stone, knocking down pins or hitting a golf ball, every action must be performed with great precision, since the object must hit a specific target, often located at a distance.

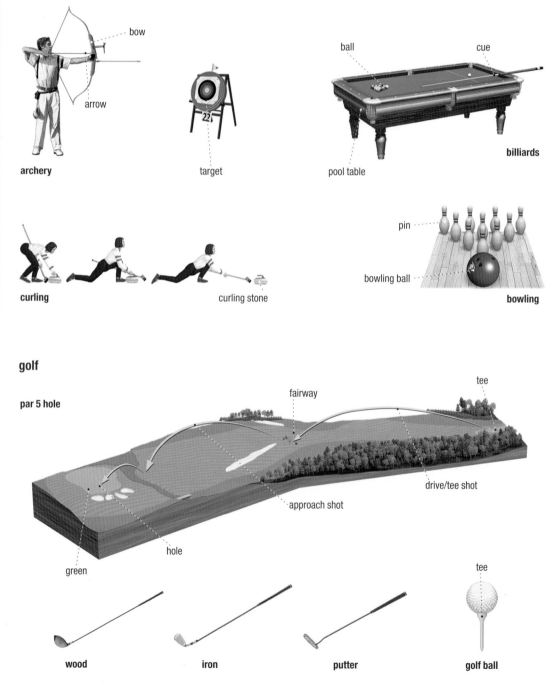

bow

archery

arrow

target

ball

cue

billiards

pool table

curling

curling stone

pin

bowling ball

bowling

Sports

golf

par 5 hole

fairway

tee

drive/tee shot

approach shot

hole

green

tee

wood

iron

putter

golf ball

Karate, boxing, wrestling and judo are combat sports that pit two athletes of matching weight against each other. The athletes need top physical and mental conditioning, and they also need exceptional skill and staying power. People who practice these sports must master their level of force.

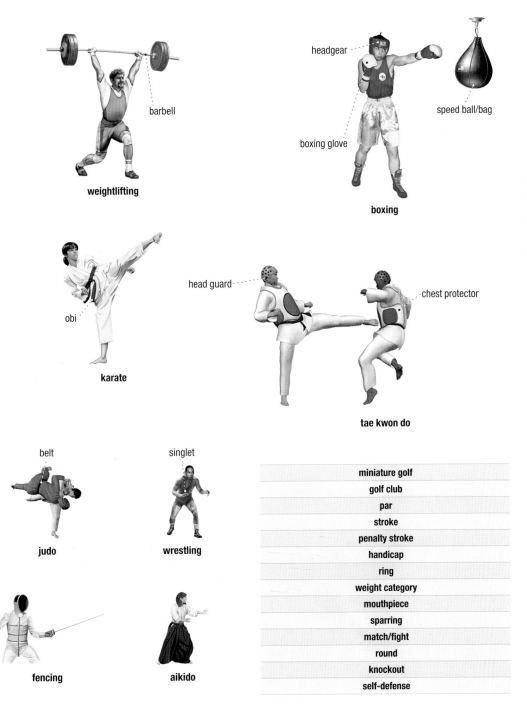

barbell

weightlifting

headgear

boxing glove

speed ball/bag

boxing

obi

karate

head guard

chest protector

tae kwon do

belt

judo

singlet

wrestling

fencing

aikido

| miniature golf |
| golf club |
| par |
| stroke |
| penalty stroke |
| handicap |
| ring |
| weight category |
| mouthpiece |
| sparring |
| match/fight |
| round |
| knockout |
| self-defense |

Sports

Whether they are on uneven terrain or a smooth track, cyclists must have a good sense of balance, excellent reflexes and great endurance. Some bicycles are made for high speed, while others are designed to overcome obstacles on rough trails. Skateboarding and in-line skating are activities that also demand great balance and perfect coordination, especially when performing acrobatics.

Sports

road racing

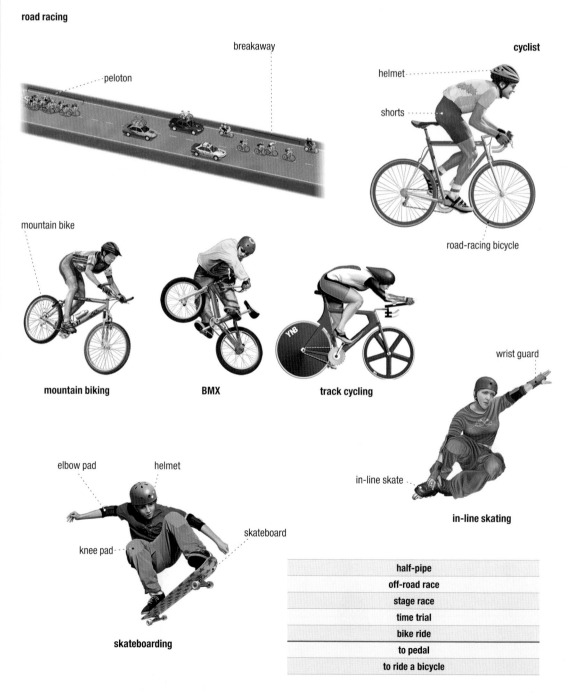

breakaway

peloton

cyclist

helmet

shorts

road-racing bicycle

mountain bike

mountain biking

BMX

track cycling

wrist guard

in-line skate

in-line skating

elbow pad

helmet

skateboard

knee pad

skateboarding

half-pipe
off-road race
stage race
time trial
bike ride
to pedal
to ride a bicycle

Mountaineering is the sport that involves climbing a mountain, natural rock face or artificial climbing structure. Aerial and mountain sports are full of risks, and require training beforehand. Use of special equipment is required for safety.

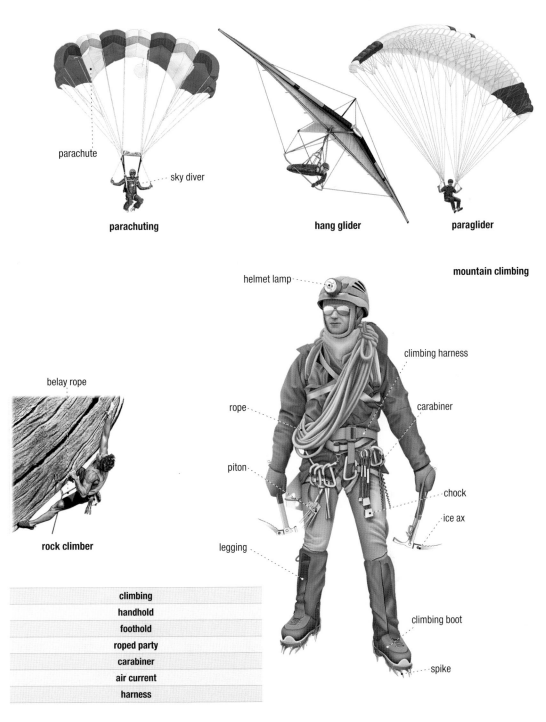

parachute

sky diver

parachuting

hang glider

paraglider

mountain climbing

helmet lamp

climbing harness

belay rope

rope

carabiner

piton

chock

ice ax

rock climber

legging

climbing boot

spike

Sports

climbing
handhold
foothold
roped party
carabiner
air current
harness

Winter sports on rinks, icy tracks or snow-covered slopes are among the fastest non-motorized sports in the world. Whether practiced alone or in teams, for recreation or competition, these sports require special equipment such as skis, skates, showshoes or luges.

ski resort

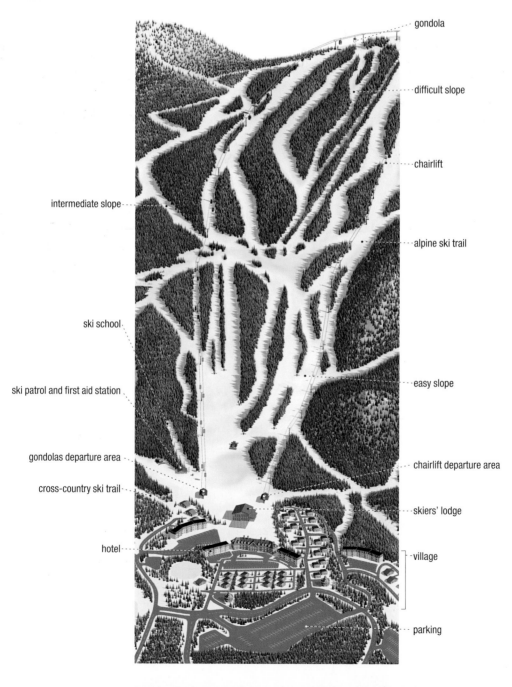

gondola

difficult slope

chairlift

intermediate slope

alpine ski trail

ski school

easy slope

ski patrol and first aid station

gondolas departure area

chairlift departure area

cross-country ski trail

skiers' lodge

hotel

village

parking

Sports

cross-country skiing

alpine skiing

skier

helmet

ski pole

ski goggles

ski pole

binding

cross-country ski

ski boot

ski

freestyle skiing

ski jumping

ice hockey

stick

skate

puck

snowboarding

speed skiing

skater

skater

figure skating

ski pass
ski lesson
ski instructor
skiing vacation
school ski trip
ski lift
beginner level
intermediate level
expert level
avalanche
sled
sliding
skating rink
I want to rent skis.

luge

snowshoe

Sports

We are surrounded by all kinds of symbols. Common symbols feature simple images that can convey a message at a glance. Easily understandable, they allow people to find things like the nearest hospital or information center. The messages conveyed by these symbols are universal and are not hampered by language barriers.

Symbols

information

women's restroom

men's restroom

wheelchair access

picnic area

trailer camping

tent camping

no camping

lodging

service station

coffee shop

restaurant

telephone

stairs

escalator

elevator

Symbols

first aid

hospital

pharmacy

police

no smoking

no photos or videos

no dogs

fire extinguisher

supermarket

automated teller machine (ATM)

currency exchange

mail

bus

train station

harbor

airport

recyclable

wireless Internet access

lost and found

taxi transport

Index

Index

B

Index